REGENTS RESTORATION DRAMA SERIES

General Editor: John Loftis

THE ORPHAN

THOMAS OTWAY

The Orphan

Edited by

ALINE MACKENZIE TAYLOR

UNIVERSITY OF NEBRASKA PRESS · LINCOLN

Publishers on the Plains

UNP

Copyright © 1976 by the University of Nebraska Press
All Rights Reserved

Library of Congress Cataloging in Publication Data

Otway, Thomas, 1652–1685.
  The orphan.

  (Regents restoration drama series)
  Based on a tale in Roger Boyle's English adventures.
Cf. Baker, Biog. dram.; Genest, Account of the English
stage, v. 1, p. 279.
  Includes bibliographical references.
  1. Taylor, Aline Mackenzie. II. Orrery, Roger
Boyle, 1st Earl of, 1621–1679. III. Title.
PR3612.07 1976   822'.4   75–13067
ISBN 0–8032–0383–7

MANUFACTURED IN THE UNITED STATES OF AMERICA

Regents Restoration Drama Series

The Regents Restoration Drama Series provides soundly edited texts, in modern spelling, of the more significant plays of the late seventeenth and early eighteenth centuries. The word "Restoration" is here used ambiguously and must be explained. A strict definition of the word would be unacceptable to everyone, for it would exclude, among many other plays, those of Congreve. If to the historian it refers to the period between 1660 and 1685 (or 1688), it has long been used by the student of drama in default of a more precise term to refer to plays belonging to the dramatic tradition established in the 1660s, weakening after 1700, and displaced in the 1730s. It is in this extended sense—imprecise though justified by academic custom—that the word is used in this series, which includes plays first produced between 1660 and 1737. Although these limiting dates are determined by political events, the return of Charles II (and the removal of prohibitions against operation of theaters) and the passage of Walpole's Stage Licensing Act, they enclose a period of dramatic history having a coherence of its own in the establishment, development, and disintegration of a tradition.

The editors have planned the series with attention to the projected dimensions of the completed whole, a representative collection of Restoration drama providing a record of artistic achievement and providing also a record of the deepest concerns of three generations of Englishmen. And thus it contains deservedly famous plays—*The Country Wife*, *The Man of Mode*, and *The Way of the World*—and also significant but little known plays, *The Virtuoso*, for example, and *City Politiques*, the former a satirical review of scientific investigation in the early years of the Royal Society, the latter an equally satiric review of politics at the time of the Popish Plot. If the volumes of famous plays finally achieve the larger circulation, the other volumes may have the greater utility, in making available texts otherwise difficult of access with the editorial apparatus needed to make them intelligible.

The editors have had the instructive example of the parallel and senior project, the Regents Renaissance Drama Series; they have in fact used the editorial policies developed for the earlier plays as their own, modifying them as appropriate for the later period and as the experience of successive editions suggested. The introductions to the separate Restoration plays differ considerably in their nature. Although a uniform body of relevant information is presented in each of them, no attempt has been made to impose a pattern of interpretation. Emphasis in the introductions has necessarily varied with the nature of the plays and inevitably—we think desirably—with the special interests and aptitudes of the different editors.

Each text in the series is based on a fresh collation of the seventeenth- and eighteenth-century editions that might be presumed to have authority. The textual notes, which appear above the rule at the bottom of each page, record all substantive departures from the edition used as the copy-text. Variant substantive readings among contemporary editions are listed there as well. Editions later than the eighteenth century are referred to in the textual notes only when an emendation originating in some one of them is received into the text. Variants of accidentals (spelling, punctuation, capitalization) are not recorded in the notes. Contracted form of characters' names are silently expanded in speech prefixes and stage directions, and, in the case of speech prefixes, are regularized. Additions to the stage directions of the copy-text are enclosed in brackets.

Spelling has been modernized along consciously conservative lines, but within the limits of a modernized text the linguistic quality of the original has been carefully preserved. Contracted preterites have regularly been expanded. Punctuation has been brought into accord with modern practices. The objective has been to achieve a balance between the pointing of the old editions and a system of punctuation which, without overloading the text with exclamation marks, semicolons, and dashes, will make the often loosely flowing verse and prose of the original syntactically intelligible to the modern reader. Dashes are regularly used only to indicate interrupted speeches, or shifts of address within a single speech.

Explanatory notes, chiefly concerned with glossing obsolete

words and phrases, are printed below the textual notes at the bottom of each page. References to stage directions in the notes follow the admirable system of the Revels editions, whereby stage directions are keyed, decimally, to the line of the text before or after which they occur. Thus, a note on 0.2 has reference to the second line of the stage direction at the beginning of the scene in question. A note on 115.1 has reference to the first line of the stage direction following line 115 of the text of the relevant scene. Speech prefixes, and any stage directions attached to them, are keyed to the first line of accompanying dialogue.

JOHN LOFTIS

Stanford University

Contents

List of Abbreviations

Bell   John Bell, ed. *The British Theatre*. London, 1776.

Ghosh   J. C. Ghosh, ed. *The Works of Thomas Otway*. 2 vols. Oxford, 1932.

Gildon   Charles Gildon. *The Laws of Poetry, as laid down by the Duke of Buckinghamshire*. London, 1721.

OED   *Oxford English Dictionary*

om.   omitted

Q1   First Quarto, 1680

Q2   Second Quarto, 1685

Q3   Third Quarto, 1691

Q4   Fourth Quarto, 1696

S.D.   stage direction

S.P.   speech prefix

W1   *The Collected Works of Mr. Thomas Otway*. London, 1712.

Introduction

The present edition of *The Orphan; or, The Unhappy Marriage*, is based on the first quarto (Q1), published in May 1680.[1] It is an unattractive little volume; but for all its crowded print, and obvious misprints, it suggests the quality of Otway's verse when it was spoken by Betterton and his friends on the stage of the Dorset Garden playhouse. It is verse designed for a style of acting that was neither naturalistic nor pantomimic, but declamatory and formal, its effect depending on the speaking voice and the diction of the actor, "the soul of lively action," as John Marston once called it.[2] The pages are littered with colloquial elisions and contractions, uncouth to the eye. Initial capitals mark the accented words; without them the verse often goes haltingly. The pointing shows little regard for conventional syntax, for it was designed to mark the actor's "breathings" and to indicate the pace of the lines. Indeed, on the printed page Otway's verse has much in common with the printed score of the arias, duets, and recitatives of opera, since its appeal is to the ear and to the emotions rather than to the eye and the intellect. As Colley Cibber observed,

> In the just delivery of poetical numbers, particularly where the sentiments are pathetick, it is scarce credible upon how minute an article of sound depends their greatest beauty or inaffection. The voice of a singer is not more strictly ty'd to time and tune, than that of an actor in theatrical elocution: the least syllable too long, or too slightly dwelt upon in a period, depreciates it to nothing; which very syllable, if rightly touch'd, shall ... give life and spirit to the whole. I · never heard a line in tragedy come from Betterton, wherein my judgment, my ear, and my imagination, were not fully satisfy'd.[3]

1. "Printed for R. Bentley, and M. Magnes, in Russel-Street in Covent-Garden, 1680."
2. Preface to *The Malcontent*.
3. Cibber, *Apology for His Own Life* (Everyman's Library), p. 62.

This effect is unfortunately lost to the present-day reader, whether or not the text is modernized.

The second quarto (Q2) was published in February 1685, two months before Otway's death on 14 April. Though it is far better than Q1 for typography, it corrects only the most obvious misprints and differs from Q1 chiefly in spelling, initial capitals, and punctuation. Some of the changes may have been made by Otway, presumably for euphony in speaking; but some new errors have been introduced by the printer, and the doubtful readings of Q1 are not elucidated. The third quarto (Q3), 1691, and the fourth quarto (Q4), 1696, indicate probable revivals of the play in those years; the changes are the sort that actors would make for greater ease in speaking Otway's lines. The principal source of corruption in the steady process of the corruption of Otway's text is *The Collected Works of Mr. Thomas Otway* (W1), published in two volumes by Jacob Tonson in 1712.

The textual notes for the present edition give the variants from Q1 that appear in Q2, and the more significant ones that appear in Q3–4 and in W1. They also give the emendations of nineteenth-century editors that J. C. Ghosh admitted into his text of *The Orphan*.[4] Stage directions which are lacking in the first four quartos have been supplied in brackets, wherever physical action is involved, from the first acting version published by John Bell in *The British Theatre* in 1776. No directions are given for tone and manner which are implied by the text or described later in detail by one of the characters.

The Orphan had its première at the Duke's Theatre in Dorset Garden sometime between Shrove Tuesday, 24 February 1680 (when the Duke and Duchess of York returned from exile in Scotland—an event which the Prologue celebrates), and Saturday, 6 March, when Pepys saw "2 acts of the New Play Orphan."[5] Apparently it had a very short run, for it was printed almost immediately and announced in the Term Catalogue for May. The publication of the second quarto in February 1685 argues a revival shortly before the death of Charles II on 6 February. There is

4. *The Works of Thomas Otway*, 2 vols. (Oxford, 1932).
5. *The London Stage*, Part I, 1660–1700, ed. William Van Lennep, with Introduction by Emmett L. Avery and Arthur Scouten (Carbondale, Ill., 1965), p. 286. All dates of performance are drawn from this work.

no further record of performance until Monday, 10 January, 1687, when the play was presented at court. Two other seventeenth-century performances are recorded, one on Tuesday, 9 February, 1692, when the Queen and the Maids of Honor were at the playhouse, and the other on Tuesday, 21 November, 1699.

In spite of a brilliant cast that included Thomas Betterton, William Smith, and Elizabeth Barry,[6] *The Orphan* made a disappointing entrance into the world. London was still in the throes of the political hysteria generated by the "Popish" plot. There were riots and disorders at the Duke's Theatre when rehearsals began in February, and the players were prohibited from acting.[7] During the interdiction, they seem to have performed a series of comedies at court, but not *The Orphan*: the court wanted diversion, the king preferred comedies, and there was quite enough "tragedy" in the everyday world outside the playhouse.

Otway offered his play as a tribute to the politically anathematized Duke of York, whose former naval victories he eulogized in the Prologue, and to the Duchess of York, to whom he dedicated the play. It does not appear that the royal patrons responded generously. The Duchess, "very much indisposed with a cold,"[8] failed to attend any of the first performances, and Otway, perhaps tactlessly, dwelt on her absence in his Dedicatory Epistle. His disappointment is understandable, for, as Nathaniel Lee said at the time, a Royal Duchess's "single Presence on the Poet's day is a Subsistence for him all the Years after."[9] Nor does it appear that she made the usual handsome present of money for the author's dedication. So much we may deduce from the bitterness of the Epistle to Bentley the publisher which Otway prefixed to *The Soldier's Fortune* six months later:

6. For a description of the cast for the première, see my *Next to Shakespeare: Otway's "Venice Preserv'd" and "The Orphan" and Their History on the London Stage* (Durham, 1950; rpt. New York, AMS Press, 1970), pp. 73–84.

7. *The True News; or, Mercurius Anglicus* (4–7 February, 1679/1680). For the riots, see *The London Stage* for February 1680. For the rehearsing of plays (usually three to four weeks), see W. J. Lawrence, *Old Theatre Days and Ways* (London, 1935), Chap. 4, esp. p. 57.

8. Newsletter, 4 March, 1680, *Calendar of State Papers, Domestic*, Charles II, 1679–80, p. 409.

9. Dedicatory Epistle to the Duchess of Richmond, prefixed to *Theodosius; or, The Force of Love* (Dorset Garden, ca. Sept. 1680).

For Mr. *Bentley*, you pay honestly for the Copy; and an Epistle to you is a sort of an Acquitance, and may be probably welcome; when to a Person of higher Rank and Order, it looks like an Obligation for Praises, which he knows he does not deserve, and therefore is very unwilling to part with ready Money for.[10]

The Latin epigraph he affixed to the title page of *The Orphan* epitomizes the bitterness of a neglected artist. It is a quotation from *The Satyricon* of Petronius Arbiter, and translated it runs thus:

The man who trusts the sea consoles himself with high profits; the man who follows war and the camp is girded with gold; the base flatterer lies drunk on a couch of purple dye; the man who tempts young wives gets money for his sin; eloquence alone shivers in rags and cold, and calls upon a neglected art with unprofitable tongue.[11]

After Otway's death, when some measure of calm had returned to the nation, playgoers recovered the serenity of temper that luxuriates in the pathos of a domestic tragedy of manners and passion. By 1780, Doctor Johnson could say:

This is one of the few plays that keep possession of the stage, and has pleased for almost a century through all the vicissitudes of dramatic fashion. Of this play nothing new can easily be said. It is a domestic tragedy drawn from middle life. Its whole power is upon the affections, for it is not written with much comprehension of thought or elegance of expression. But if the heart is interested, many other beauties may be wanting, yet not missed.[12]

Not a word about the "immorality" and "profaneness" which Jeremy Collier excoriated in 1698, when he fulminated against

10. *The Complete Works of Thomas Otway,* ed. Montague Summers (London, 1926), 2:237.

11. *Satyricon,* chap. 83, trans. Michael Heseltine (Loeb Classics), p. 166.

12. Samuel Johnson, *Lives of the Poets,* ed. G. B. Hill (Oxford, 1905), 1:245.

the "smut" Monimia is made to speak, and against Chamont's irreverent treatment of the clergy![13] One can only surmise that Doctor Johnson's judgment was suffused with his lingering memory of the enchantment David Garrick cast over the play in 1747, when he impersonated Chamont to the Castalio of Spranger Barry and the Monimia of Mrs. Cibber, one of the greatest casts that ever appeared in *The Orphan*.[14]

When Johnson wrote, *The Orphan* had already reached the peak of its popularity with playgoers. Critics voiced their well-considered objections. *The Morning Chronicle* for 8–10 March, 1757, found that "the Circumstance on which the Catastrophe turns is gross and shocking." The Dramatic Censor for 1770 concluded his survey of *The Orphan* by deeming the play "highly censurable," "sincerely lamenting such a vile prostitution of Otway's masterly talents," and most sincerely wishing it "banished by general consent, both from the closet and the stage."[15] The world which had given shape to *The Orphan* was passing: Edmund Burke wrote its obsequies in 1790 when he heard of the sack of Versailles and the savagery of the mob of *sans culottes* in the streets of Paris. "The age of chivalry is gone," he said.

That of sophisters, economists, and calculators, has succeeded. . . . It is gone, that sensibility of principle, that chastity of honour, which felt a stain like a wound . . . which ennobled whatever it touched, and under which vice itself lost half its evil, by losing all its grossness.[16]

Burke's views on the "sensibility of principle" and "chastity of honour" were not shared by the majority of nineteenth-century playgoers. Before the Regency came to an end, *The Orphan* had been banished from the stage, along with the gay comedies of

13. *A Short View of the Immorality and Profaneness of the English Stage* (London, 1698), pp. 9, 146, 100, 101.

14. At the time, Johnson was in close touch with the playhouse: in 1747, Garrick assumed the management of Drury Lane Theatre, and Johnson wrote the Prologue for the opening on Tuesday, 15 September. Two years later Garrick produced Johnson's play *Irene* (6 Feb. 1749).

15. Francis Gentleman, *The Dramatic Censor; or, Critical Companion* (London, 1770), 2:60.

16. *Reflections on the Revolution in France*, in *The Works of Edmund Burke* (Oxford World's Classics), 4:83.

Congreve and Etherege and the saturnine comedies of Wycherley. One old fogy, however, confessed that "bookworms keep them in their closets, away from young people." Toward the end of the century, Sir Edmund Gosse read *The Orphan* quietly in his "closet" and found the play marred not so much by "the indelicacy of the main situation" as by the "many faults in the construction of [the] plot":

> The foolish pretence of Castalio, the want of perception shown by Monimia, the impossible and ruffianly crime of Polydore—for which no just preparation is made in the sketch of his character—all these are radical faults which go near to destroy the probability of the story.[17]

Other critics raised even stronger objections to Polydore, finding it impossible to reconcile the reprehensible yet understandable "libertine" (viz. "villain") with the remorseful penitent who atones for his "crime" by suicide. "Poor and unsufficiently motived in plot" was the verdict of the critic for *The Christian Science Monitor* (28 May, 1925) after he had been present at the revival given by the Phoenix Society, "since a dozen frank words from any one of the characters would have ended the drama."

In short, these later critics objected to the motivation of *The Orphan*, or more precisely to that formative element which Aristotle called "ethos" and the seventeenth-century dramatic theorists "manners"—"the Causes and Principles of Action," as Jeremy Collier defined it,[18] but not quite that "second nature" which William of Wykeham understood when he gave to his foundations at Winchester and Oxford the precept "Manners Makyth Man." The legacy of a chivalric age, "this mixed system of opinion and sentiment" (which Burke extolled) had already moved some distance from its informing spirit of "trouthe and honour, fredom and curteisie" before it crystallized in the external forms of behavior observed at the court of the first Stuarts, the rationale of these forms not to be examined too closely by

17. *Seventeenth-Century Studies* (London, 1885), p. 299.
18. *Short View of the Immorality and Profaneness of the English Stage*, in *Critical Essays of the Seventeenth Century*, ed. J. E. Spingarn (Oxford, 1909), 3:282. See also John Dryden, Preface to *Troilus and Cressida*, in *Essays*, ed. W. P. Ker, 1:213–14.

anyone who sought preferment. After the restoration of Charles II, the forms survived, more relaxed perhaps, but the inconsistencies and contradictions that had invaded their "causes and principles" were becoming apparent. It was indeed a world of antinomies. The Earl of Rochester followed profligacy with the thoughtfulness of a philosopher, but on his deathbed turned to theology and the ministrations of Bishop Burnet. The Earl of Essex, whose "piety" Evelyn commended, cut his throat in the Tower like a Stoic, to the wonderment of his peers. Margaret Blagge, Maid of Honor to the Queen, set all her mind on salvation as she played the part of Diana in the Great Court Masque of *Calisto*, weighted down with jewels worth £20,000. The Great Duke of Ormonde, assailed on all sides by enemies at court, remained unswervingly loyal to the King; but the equally loyal Duke of Newcastle, finding no meed of honor at court, withdrew to his country house. And all the while politicians sought their own interest, encouraged by bribes from the French king; the royal mistresses grew rich; and the bend sinister was honored at court. "Oh! it was a naughty Court," George Meredith wrote in Chapter 2 of *The Egoist*:

> Yet have we dreamed of it as the period when an English cavalier was grace incarnate; far from the boor now hustling us in another sphere; beautifully mannered, every gesture dulcet. And if the ladies were . . . we will hope they have been traduced. But if they were, if they were too tender, ah! gentlemen were gentlemen then—worth perishing for! There is this dream in the English country; and it must be an aspiration after some form of melodious gentlemanliness which is imagined to have inhabited the island at one time; as among our poets the dream of the period of a circle of chivalry here is encouraged for the pleasure of the imagination.[19]

The "radical faults" which Gosse observed in *The Orphan* suggest the now obvious dissonances inherent in the material from which Otway drew his fable. The plot of *The Orphan* turns on a single situation which is precipitated by three deliberate deceptions; it veils rape and incest. For the theme Otway had

19. George Meredith, *The Egoist* (1879), p. 20; also ed. Angus Wilson (Signet Classics), p. 18.

dramatic precedents in the story of Mithridates, which Lee had recently reworked; in the story of Oedipus, which Dryden and Lee refurbished in collaboration; and above all in the well-known story of Lucrece, which Lee was to present in *Lucius Junius Brutus*.[20] For his treatment of the theme, however, Otway had no precedent. Into a plot that culminates in rape and incest and concludes with three suicides, he has introduced a motif of deception proper to comedy. Parallels to Polydore's deception of Monimia can be found in such classical comedies as the *Menaechmi*, the *Adelphi*, and the *Amphitryon*; in Shakespeare's bitter comedies, *All's Well* and *Measure for Measure*; and in Fletcher's *Scornful Lady*. In the comedies the motif is used to laugh a victim out of countenance or to cut Gordian knots in the plot. The main action of *The Orphan* is thus compounded out of a stock motif of comedy and one of the most terrible themes of tragedy.

In the conception of this central situation there is a fundamental dissonance. A deception perpetrated in the spirit of jest turns out to be a crime from which the principals recoil in horror, and the juxtaposition of the two elements is disconcerting enough to shatter the illusion of reality. Or rather, it puts the burden of maintaining the illusion on the audience as well as on the actor, for it entails a violent shift in the point of view from which the action is to be seen, and the audience must be able to slip easily from one point of view to the other—or lose all illusion of probability. That willing suspension of disbelief lasts only so long as the unstated assumptions which motivate the action of the play are the unstated assumptions which the audience bring to it—unstated assumptions which, if they do not entirely share, they at least acquiesce in as the way of the world.

Otway did not invent the plot of *The Orphan*; he followed the general outline of the story which is found in *The History of Brandon*, Part I of *The English Adventures*, written presumably by Roger Boyle, Earl of Orrery, and published in May 1676.[21] But in taking over the story of Brandon for his plot, Otway inevitably made some changes. For example, Brandon, the narrator of the

20. *Mithridates*, Drury Lane, Feb. 1678; *Oedipus*, Dorset Garden, ca. Nov. 1678; *Lucius Junius Brutus*, Dorset Garden, Dec. 1680.

21. Reprinted in part by Montague Summers in *The Complete Works of Thomas Otway* (London, 1926), 2:313–20. All quotations are from this edition.

tragic episode, is no longer the central figure in the action, but, transformed into Polydore, shares prominence with the elder brother, the heroine, and her brother. The sketchily drawn, rather mercenary father becomes the fully developed Acasto, the open-handed, high-minded, but disillusioned exponent of a loyalist philosophy of life and politics. The two new characters who are introduced, a brother for the heroine and a sister for the twin-heroes, create new complications that fill up gaps in a plot that must extend for five acts. A loquacious page keeps the plot moving by informing one or the other of the principals of everything he spies on.[22] The most striking change in the action, however, is to be found at the end, for Otway kills off three of his principal characters by suicide, whereas the author of *Brandon* allowed two of his principals to die merely by languishing, and sent the narrator off to the Continent to expiate his sin by deeds of desperate valor—only to return at last to take possession of his father's estate. Furthermore, Otway introduced a confession of the crime, after the style of Roman Lucrece; Polydore confesses—he even writes out a full account to be read after his death. In the narrative it is doubtful whether the elder brother ever learns the truth; the whole affair is regarded as an unintentional crime, a fatal mistake, that only silence can remedy.

Many of the changes that Otway made in *The History of Brandon* result from his recasting the story in a dramatic mould. For Otway, this mould was provided by certain of the plays of Beaumont and Fletcher, tempered by the fashionable manners of the Restoration.[23] Acasto, the old soldier-courtier now in retirement, is reminiscent of Archas in *The Loyal Subject*, a part in which Betterton as a young actor had distinguished himself.[24] The younger brother Polydore has a namesake in that earlier Polydore in *The Mad Lover*, a play which Pepys saw at least three times

22. At a later date, a page (or a waiting woman) was required to take care of the heroine's train; Cordelio and Florella thus serve a double function.

23. For other influences which have been suggested, seen Bonamy Dobrée, *Restoration Tragedy* (Oxford, 1929); R. G. Ham, *Otway and Lee* (New Haven, 1931).

24. John Downes, *Roscius Anglicanus* (1708), p. 18. Acasto has been compared to Belarius in *Cymbeline* (Ham, *Otway and Lee*, p. 144), a play "improved" by Thomas D'Urfey and produced as *The Injured Princess; or, The Fatal Wager* (Drury Lane, ca. March 1682). Acasto, however, has a fine

because he admired Betterton in the part of the elder brother, the "mad lover."[25] The closing scene of that play is noteworthy: the two brothers live up to their pact of friendship and debate which of them shall have the lady, each deferring with obstinate courtesy to the other.

The principal characters of *The Orphan* bear an even more notable resemblance to those of *The Maid's Tragedy*. There are the sharply contrasted twin-heroes—the gay rake Polydore, whose intentions are perhaps a shade more honorable than those of Amintor's King, and the uncertain-tempered Castalio, who recalls the weak and brooding Amintor; and there is the soldier-brother of the heroine—Chamont, whose explosive temper matches that of Melantius, the bluff, downright brother of Evadne. The resemblance is heightened by the relationships which Otway establishes among his four principal characters. In both plays the heroine stands at the apex of a triangle, her affections sought by two rivals of contrasting temper, the one rakish, the other sentimental and ineffecutal; in both a blunt soldier-brother interferes in her affairs and opposes one of her suitors. In both plays there is the same morbid atmosphere emanating from a morally distorted central situation—with one notable difference. Monimia is as virtuous as Evadne is vicious, for Otway has carefully followed the advice of his own Lady Squeamish:

> Oh Cousin, if you undertake to write a Tragedy, take my Counsel: Be sure to say soft melting tender things in it, that may be moving, and make your Ladies Characters vertuous whatere you do.[26]

Finally, there is an unmistakable resemblance to *The Maid's Tragedy* in the manner of Polydore's suicide, for he provokes a duel with Castalio and runs on his brother's sword, very much as

---

house in the country—in Bohemia, as Archas has in Muscovy, both equally remote from the cave in Roman Britain where Belarius lives with his two "supposed" sons, one of them known as Polydore. See also Arthur Colby Sprague, *Beaumont and Fletcher on the Restoration Stage* (New Haven, 1931).

25. Pepys's *Diary*, 9 Feb. and 2 Dec. 1661; 18 Feb. 1669; also John Downes, *Roscius Anglicanus*, p. 18. On 11 Oct. 1675, Nell Gwynn saw a performance of *The Mad Lover*.

26. *Friendship in Fashion*, III.i.145–48.

Aspatia, disguised as a boy and claiming to be her own brother, provokes Amintor to a duel and lets herself be killed. In 1762, Lord Kames demonstrated the propriety of Polydore's action with all the legal subtlety of the Scots judge that he was:

> Polydore's crime, in his own opinion, merited that judgment [of death]; and justice was satisfied, when he fell by the hand of the man he had injured; he wanted, at the same time to punish his brother for breach of faith; and he could not do this more effectually, than by betraying his brother to be his executioner.[27]

It may be easier for us to believe that in contriving Polydore's suicide Otway had his eye on Aspatia, for *The Maid's Tragedy* was one of the more popular plays in the repertory of the Theatre Royal, if we believe Thomas Rymer, who in 1677 ascribed its success to the excellence of Hart and Mohun in the Quarrel Scene in Act III.[28] Two years later, Dryden remarked that the last scene in his own *Troilus and Cressida* was "hinted to me by Mr. Betterton," and that it was "an imitation of the scene betwixt Brutus and Cassius," or of "the faulty copy of it in Amintor and Melantius."[29] Betterton, as Manager of the Duke's Company, kept a sharp eye on the stage successes at the Theatre Royal, and quarrel scenes between friends being popular, Otway has provided several in *The Orphan*, all of them conducted with great punctilio. Furthermore, the success of *Othello* at the Theatre Royal suggests that secret marriages ending in suicide were also popular, especially with the Queen and the Maids of Honor. At Dorset Garden, however, *Romeo and Juliet* caught on only after Otway "improved" it as *Caius Marius*, setting the action against the background of the civil wars between Marius and Sulla in Republican Rome. Suicide for a Christian of sound mind was still anathematized by the Church and penalized by the Law; Moors and antique Romans were excused as being unenlightened pagans. The triple suicide that brings *The Orphan* to a close is therefore the more remarka-

27. Henry Home, Lord Kames, *Elements of Criticism* (Edinburgh, 1762), pp. 74–75.
28. *Tragedies of the Last Age Considered* (London, 1678; licensed 17 July 1677), pp. 138–39.
29. *The Essays of John Dryden*, ed. W. P. Ker (Oxford, 1926), 1:204–5.

ble, set as it is in a context of sacramental marriage, of chapel-going, and of statements about self-examination, confession, and absolution.

By introducing new characters and consequently new episodes into the simple action of *Brandon*, Otway was obliged to introduce new motives, and thereby risk obscuring the simple motivation of his source. At the beginning of his narrative, Brandon says:

> That many men run into high crimes designedly, cannot be a greater truth than it is, that others fall into them both against their inclinations and intentions . . . . This I know, that the crime I fell into was not so much my sin, as it is my punishment.

Brandon repudiates all moral responsibility for his unwitting sin. His elder brother has not deceived him, but he has failed to confide in him—for a very simple reason: their father would never consent to a marriage with Victoria, whose "Beauty and Virtue was all her Portion"; and he is unwilling to involve his younger brother in the shake-up he knows will follow upon the discovery of his marriage. Brandon, unlike Polydore, is unaware of his brother's feelings for Victoria; like Polydore, he does not suspect his brother's marriage; like Polydore again, he overhears what he thinks is an assignation, and overwhelmed by a sudden impulse of jealousy, he takes his brother's place. On her death-bed, Victoria points out to him his real motive: "You thought that I had been unchaste, and that gave you the right to be so."

The Orphan is written in the light of no such clear-cut ideas. Polydore confronts his brother on two separate occasions: he and Castalio are quite aware of each other's feelings for Monimia, and Polydore is deceived by his brother's firm assurance that he has no intention of marrying Monimia—for Castalio has a notion that if he can gain time he can present the world with a *fait accompli* and reconcile his brother to it afterwards. The Count de Grammont and Voltaire would not have boggled at Castalio's "duplicity"; they would have understood it as the refined art of using "a false confidence to disguise a real treachery" in the game of love.[30] An early critic took a more complaisant view. He saw only

30. Anthony Hamilton, *Memoirs of the Count de Grammont*, trans. Horace Walpole, with Introduction and Notes by Sir Walter Scott (New York, 1889), chap. 4, p. 64; Voltaire, *Oeuvres Complètes* (Paris, 1879), 24:204–8.

that Castalio was caught in the conventional conflict of love and friendship with courtesy:

> In this Manner [of friendship] did they live, till *Monimia* having confest an Affection for *Castalio*, he feared to wound his Brother with Intelligence so unwelcome, and from that Time began to be more reserved in speaking of her.[31]

Only an actor of the calibre of Robert Wilks could have persuaded a well-bred playgoer that the considerate reticence of a gentleman is not duplicity, for the line between the two is not always easy to draw. Wilks had made his mark in the role of Amintor before he attempted Castalio; he excelled in portraying "sorrow, tenderness, or resignation," [32] and his graceful address and elegant delicacy of manner won his "spectators' most generous approbation."[33] He was fortunate in having as his Polydore an actor of equal stature, Barton Booth, a tragedian who had modelled his style on Betterton's and who found his proper métier in portraying "the more turbulent transports of the heart."[34] Yet playhouse tradition has it that Polydore "from the spirit and gaiety which Booth knew how to throw into [the part], was esteemed the principal character in the play" and that since Booth's day "no man has had the good fortune to impose so happily on an audience in Polydore."[35] His "gay libertine air" set the right note for the Castalio of Wilks to "[talk] as he talked and [grant] all he asked" (II.359)—and just the right contrast for "the peculiar art" Wilks had of "enforcing a tender meaning, by his soft and dewy manner of shedding it into the ear."[36]

From the printed text, however, Castalio's reasons for evasion, and for the concealment of his marriage, are now hard to under-

31. *The Dramatic Historiographer* (1735), p. 222.

32. Cibber, *Apology*, p. 294. Wilks and Booth are recorded as playing together in these roles between 1707 and 1718. Their Chamonts reduced the part to that of a bully, and their Monimias were not distinguished.

33. Thomas Davies, *Dramatic Miscellanies* (London, 1784), 3:206.

34. Cibber, *Apology*, p. 296.

35. Thomas Davies, *Memoirs of the Life of David Garrick, Esq.* (London, 1808), 1:53.

36. Aaron Hill, letter dated 9 Feb. 1731 (*Works* [London, 1753], 1:32).

stand, unless he assumes that their father Acasto would forbid his marriage with Monimia and take steps to prevent it; though Acasto voices no opposition, everyone seems to assume that he would oppose the marriage—Castalio (II.356–61), the Chaplain (III.216–21, 251–53), Monimia (IV.60–61, 341–46), Chamont (II.147–293). And Polydore too, for when he and Castalio talk of their great desire to go to the wars, and their vexation at Acasto's refusal, Castalio says, "I could not do a thing to cross his will!" (I.113). The remark at once puts Polydore in mind of Monimia and the state of his brother's feelings for her. When he asks pointedly, "You would not wed Monimia, would you?" (I.157), Castalio walks into the trap prepared for him by time-honored convention. In wealthy families, marriages for love were the exception; marriages were arranged by parents or guardians, not always to the liking of the persons involved. The anomalous "double standard," however, tolerated a young gentleman's sowing a few wild oats, if the ladies were willing.

Yet, if Acasto opposes the marriage of his son and heir with the dowerless orphan who is his ward as strongly as he opposes his sons' going to the wars, he gladly consents to the marriage of her equally penniless brother Chamont to his daughter Serina. His consent to Chamont's marriage would seem to nullify his opposition to Monimia's. Indeed, Chamont's blunt directness in seeking Acasto's consent to his wooing and winning of Serina shows up all the more sharply the evasiveness of Castalio in concealing his marriage from everyone, and especially from Polydore. Unfortunately, a "few frank words" from Castalio would have brought the tragedy to an end in the first act, if what Polydore says at the close of the play is to be believed (V.445–47). This is the pitfall Otway dug for himself when he recast the story of Brandon in dramatic form. Only by creating an impression of strong forces arrayed against Castalio and Monimia could he divert playgoers' attention from the difficulty. Fortunate for his play that playgoers recognized the conventions and understood that an obstacle to the marriage of Castalio and Monimia existed, where none existed to the marriage of Chamont and Serina, which was "approved" if not "arranged."

By all the rules of the code of honor and its double standard, Acasto should have opposed the marriage of his elder son with a dowerless orphan, however high born. But Acasto is as full of contradictions as King Lear himself.[37] He excoriates the court, but celebrates the king's birthday with festivities. He speaks of his dead lady with the greatest tenderness, but warns his sons against marriage. He remembers his own feats of gallantry as a soldier and praises Chamont for his bravery, but obstinately refuses his own sons permission to seek their fortunes in war. There cling to him all the high chivalry and romance of the Cavaliers who rode out on their hopeless missions for Charles I—and all the disillusionment they endured after the restoration of Charles II. Moreover, he flouts all the precedents of Common Law concerning the inheritance of property, for he divides his estate equally among his two sons and Chamont; and he provides a dowry for Monimia, but none for his daughter Serina. "Go to," he tells his sons, "y'are fools, and know me not" (II.52), and with that remark we must heartily agree. Small wonder that eighteenth-century playgoers confessed they had never seen the part well done, though they remembered that it had been done formerly "by the old lyons."[38] The great American actor-manager, William Burke Wood, recognized that the part of Acasto is among "the old men of the stage, requiring great study and labor," and "among high efforts in pure tragedy."[39]

The motivation of the plot of *The Orphan* grows out of conventions and attitudes of mind which make up the climate of opinion of the early 1670s, before the Popish panic diverted playwrights' attention from heroic sentiment to matters of topical interest. The heroic-Platonic conventions in the play, as well as their negation, are noticeable:[40] Castalio's pact of friendship with Polydore in the pursuit of Monimia—which he never meant to keep; and Chamont's recognition of the code of honor which precludes his sister's marriage with either of her benefactor's sons,[41] and which

37. *King Lear* was performed at Dorset Garden on Tuesday, 29 June 1675, and again about March 1681, "Revis'd with Alterations" by Nahum Tate.
38. *Theatrical Examiner* (London, 1757), p. 82; *Theatrical Review* (London, 1772), 1:79.
39. *Personal Recollections of the Stage* (Philadelphia, 1855), pp. 321, 328.
40. For these conventions, see Kathleen M. Lynch, *The Social Mode of Restoration Comedy* (New York, 1926), pp. 44, 80, et passim.
41. Cf. the story of Miss Grimani's refusal to marry Viscount Andover (the son of her benefactors), told by Julian Young in *A Memoir of Charles Mayne Young* (London, 1871), 1:29.

consequently makes a liaison the danger he must protect her from. Castalio's offering Monimia to Polydore has a curious parallel in the story Gilbert Burnet tells of the Duchess of Orleans (d. 1670);[42] and Chamont's warning Monimia against Castalio and his promises acquires new interest in the light of contemporary gossip about fake marriages.[43] These episodes conjure up the atmosphere of the Court of England in the days of the Count de Grammont.

The atmosphere of court corruption pervades the play; it is strangely at odds with the pastoral setting. The old cavalier Acasto has fled to this retreat to escape the evils that disgust him, yet he speaks of them on so many occasions that one can only conclude that he has brought with him some of the corruption he detests. But indeed only this emphasis on court corruption could make his rustic retreat credible, for in 1680 no one fled to the country for sheer love of it. Acasto binds the play together. He is redoubtable as the head of a noble house, and yet he finds himself opposed by everyone except Serina and Polydore, who seems to be his favorite. Secluded in the country and kept idle with country sports and music, Polydore has still acquired "all the arts of fine persuasion" that distinguished the gay rakes at the court of Charles II. He has already seduced the Page's sister; and the Page is so knowing in tricks and wiles, and is so accomplished a tale-bearer, that one would expect to find him on the backstairs at Whitehall rather than in a stately country house where a man like Acasto is master. Castalio too has perfected all the fine gentleman's arts of skillful evasion. He knows quite as well as Polydore the convention which distinguishes between a wife and a mistress, which tolerates a liaison but opposes a marriage between a son and heir and a dowerless orphan. Wealth is the obstacle the world would place in the way of his marriage to Monimia; and wealth is spoken of constantly in the play, though it is masked by "honor," and veiled by "all the pleasing illusions" and "all the decent drapery" that can be furnished from the wardrobe of

42. *History of His Own Time* (London, 1818), 1:337–38.

43. Cf. the story of the Earl of Oxford and "Roxana" (identified with the actress Mrs. Davenport, fl. 1662), told by Anthony Hamilton in *Memoirs of the Count de Grammont*, pp. 275–76; and by Madame D'Aulnoy in *Memoirs of the Court of England*, trans. Mrs. William Henry Arthur (London, 1913), pp. 269–80.

elegant manners.[44] Since everyone tacitly assumes that there can
be no question of marriage between Castalio and Monimia, then
marriage ought to be out of the question; since Monimia's position renders her vulnerable to a liaison, and since she seems willing to play a hole-and-corner game with Castalio, Polydore, with
his brother's assurance, assumes that they are both in pursuit of a
game of love, something comparable to the boar hunt they have
just engaged in, and nothing more. Chamont assumes the same,
assured by the dream his conventional mind has conjured up and
his chance meeting with a "witch." Thereafter he makes a nui-
sance of himself in his determination to protect Monimia, and,
when she contracts a secret marriage, to have it recognized at
once. Castalio, bent on contracting an "unapproved" marriage for
love, recognizes the menace to it offered by the ideals of Acasto
and Chamont on the one hand and those of Polydore on the
other. A hasty secret marriage, a *fait accompli*, he thinks is his only
way out of the dilemma, for everyone in the play believes that
marriage is a sacrament, the sanctity of "the word of honor"
ratified in Heaven as well as enforced by law, and once consum-
mated, irreversible. By some strange distortion worked on Christian belief by pagan Stoic notions, the marriage vow like the word
of honor can be absolved only by death; but only the Stoic assumed that death should come by suicide.

It is neither Castalio's "Fatal Love" nor his notion that he has
been "betrayed to love and all its little follies" (II.317) that de-
stroys him, along with his brother and Monimia. He is betrayed to
fashionable ideas and conventions by paying lip-service to them,
although they are at variance with his nature. The tragedy of *The
Orphan* is precipitated by a character who tries to defy the conventions that are accepted by his associates, and to shield himself
behind these conventions in order to defy them. Convention thus
assumes the external force of Fate, which, in the terms of the
play, is the compelling force of that unexamined medly of incon-
sistent ideas which constituted "the causes and principles of action" in seventeenth-century manners. For this reason, the
present-day reader will find *The Orphan* more intelligible, its
pathos and passion more tragic, if it is read, not as a decadent
Heroic Tragedy, or as a Domestic Tragedy, or as a Pathetic

44. *The Works of Edmund Burke* (Oxford World's Classics), 4:84.

Tragedy, or as a She-Tragedy—though indeed it is all of these-
—but as a Tragedy of Manners.

ALINE MACKENZIE TAYLOR

Tulane University

THE ORPHAN

Qui pelago credit, magno se faenore tollit; qui pugnas et castra petit, praecingitur auro; vilis adulator picto jacet ebrius ostro, et qui sollicitat nuptas, ad praemia peccat: sola pruinosis horret faecundia pannis atque inopi lingua desertas invocat artes.

Petron[*ius*] *Arb*[*iter*] *Sat*[*yricon*].

This epigraph is translated and discussed in the Introduction, p. xvi above.

To Her Royal Highness
The Duchess

MADAM,

After having a great while wished to write something that might be worthy to lay at Your Highness's feet, and finding it impossible: since the world has been so kind to me to judge of this poem to my advantage, as the most 5 pardonable fault which I have made in its kind, I had sinned against myself if I had not chosen this opportunity to implore what my ambition is most fond of—your favor and protection.

For though fortune would not so far bless my en- 10 deavors as to encourage them with Your Royal Highness's presence when this came into the world, yet I cannot but declare it was my design and hopes it might have been your divertisement in that happy season when you returned again to cheer all those eyes that had be- 15 fore wept for your departure, and enliven all hearts that had drooped for your absence. When wit ought to have paid its choicest tributes in, and joy have known no limits, then I hoped my little mite would not have been rejected; though my ill fortune was too hard for me, and I 20 lost a greater honor by Your Royal Highness's absence than all the applauses of the world besides can make me reparation for.

Nevertheless, I thought myself not quite unhappy so long as I had hopes, this way, yet to recompense my 25

0.2. *the Duchess*] Mary Beatrice Anne Margaret Isabel of Modena (1658–1718), only daughter of Alfonso IV of Este, Duke of Modena. She was married by proxy to James, Duke of York, on 30 September 1673, and landed at Dover on 21 November.

15–16. *returned . . . departure*] The Duke and Duchess of York had been banished first to Flanders (4 March 1679), and then to Scotland (27 October 1679). They returned to London on 24 February 1680.

19–23. *rejected . . . reparation for*] It was customary for the recipient of a dedication to attend the playhouse on the third day of performance, the poet's day, when the proceeds from the performance were paid to the playwright.

25. *this way*] by the printed dedication. The usual gratuity for a dedication was twenty guineas.

3

disappointment past. When I considered also that poetry might claim right to a little share in your favor, for Tasso and Ariosto, some of the best, have made their names eternal by transmitting to after ages the glory of your ancestors; and under the spreading of that shade, where 30 two of the best have planted their laurels, how honored should I be, who am the worst, if but a branch might grow for me.

I dare not think of offering at anything in this address that might look like a panegyric, for fear lest, when I 35 have done my best, the world should condemn me for saying too little; and you yourself check me for meddling with a task unfit for my talent.

For the description of virtues and perfections so rare as yours are ought to be done by as deliberate as skilful a 40 hand. The features must be drawn very fine to be like; hasty daubing would but spoil the picture and make it so unnatural as must want false lights to set it off. And your virtue can receive no more luster from praises than your beauty can be improved by art; which, as it charms the 45 bravest Prince that ever amazed the world with his virtue, so let but all other hearts inquire into themselves and then judge how it ought to be praised.

Your love too (as none but that great hero who has it could deserve it and, therefore, by a particular lot from 50 Heaven was destined to so extraordinary a blessing, so matchless for itself, and so wondrous for its constancy) shall be remembered to your immortal honor when all other transactions of the age you live in shall be forgotten. 55

But I forget that I am to ask pardon for the fault I have been all this while committing. Wherefore, I beg

---

27–28. *Tasso and Ariosto*] Torquato Tasso (1544–95), author of the pastoral *Aminta* (1573) and the epic *Jerusalem Delivered* (1575). He entered the service of Cardinal Luigi d'Este and during his later years was protected by Alfonso II, Duke of Ferrara. Ludovico Ariosto (1474–1533), like Tasso, spent the greater part of his life at Ferrara in the service first of Cardinal Ippolito d'Este, to whom he dedicated *Orlando Furioso* (1532), and later of Duke Alfonso d'Este.

34. *offering at*] attempting.

46–47. *virtue*] manliness, strength, bravery.

4

Your Highness to forgive this presumption, and that you will be pleased to think well of one who cannot help resolving with all the actions of life to endeavor to de- 60 serve it. Nay more, I would beg and hope it may be granted that I may, through yours, never want an advocate in his favor, whose heart and mind you have so entire a share in. It is my only portion and my fortune. I cannot but be happy so long as I have but hopes I may 65 enjoy it; and I must be miserable should it ever be my ill fate to lose it.

This, with eternal wishes for Your Royal Highness's content, happiness, and prosperity, in all humility is presented by 70

Your most obedient and devoted servant,

THO[MAS] OTWAY

---

62. *through yours*] through your favor. Otway had dedicated *Don Carlos* to the Duke in 1676.

THE PERSONS REPRESENTED IN THE TRAGEDY

Men

ACASTO, a nobleman retired
from court and living
privately in the country   *Mr. Gillow*

CASTALIO ⎫   *Mr. Betterton*
POLYDORE ⎬ his sons   *Mr. Jo. Williams*

CHAMONT, a young soldier
of fortune   *Mr. Smith*

ERNESTO ⎫ servants in the   *Mr. Norris*
PAULINO ⎬ family   *Mr. Wiltshire*

CORDELIO, Polydore's page   *The Little Girl*

CHAPLAIN   *Mr. Percival*

Women

MONIMIA, The Orphan, left under
the guardianship of old
Acasto   *Mrs. Barry*

SERINA, Acasto's daughter   *Mrs. Butler*

FLORELLA, Monimia's woman   *Mrs. Osborn*

SERVANTS, ATTENDANTS, ETC.

Scene: *Bohemia*

Servants, Attendants, etc.] In view of the furor in the world of politics, I suspect this play was first produced with every possible economy. Walk-on actors, attendants, and such received 5*s.* every acting day; with Ernesto, Paulino, the Page, and Florella—and possibly the Chaplain—there would be no great need for extras.

6

PROLOGUE

To you, great judges in this writing age,
The sons of wit, and patrons of the stage;
With all those humble thoughts, which still have swayed
His pride, much doubting, trembling and afraid
Of what is to his want of merit due,   5
And awed by every excellence in you:
The author sends to beg you would be kind,
And spare those many faults you needs must find.
You, to whom wit a common foe is grown,
The thing ye scorn, and publicly disown;   10
Though now perhaps y'are here for other ends,
He swears to me ye ought to be his friends;
For he ne'er called ye yet insipid tools,
Nor wrote one line to tell you ye were fools,
But says of wit ye have so large a store,   15
So very much, you never will have more.
He ne'er with libel treated yet the town,
The names of honest men debaubed and shown;
Nay, never once lampooned the harmless life
Of suburb virgin, or of city wife.   20
Satire's the effect of poetry's disease,
Which, sick of a lewd age, she vents for ease;
But now her only strife should be to please,
Since of ill fate the baneful cloud's withdrawn,
And happiness again begins to dawn;   25
Since back with joy and triumph he is come,
That always drove fears hence, ne'er brought 'em home.

---

11. *other ends*] alluding to the recent disturbances at the Duke's Theatre, inspired by hostility to the Duke of York and his supporters.

17. *libel*] the flood of "horrid and impudent" pamphlets that followed upon Titus Oates's "exposure" of the Popish Plot (October 1678). Otway had been the victim of a lampoon, circulated anonymously in October 1677, but written by his former patron, the Earl of Rochester, to whom he had dedicated *Titus and Berenice* (Term Catalogue, February 1677). See Appendix A.

20. *suburb . . . city*] Gibes at the Whiggish "cits" were part of the stock in trade of the Tory satirists. Cf. Epilogue, l. 8.

24. *cloud's withdrawn*] the return of the Duke of York from banishment on 24 February 1680.

Oft has he ploughed the boist'rous ocean o'er,
Yet ne'er more welcome to the longing shore,
Not when he brought home victories before;   30
For then fresh laurels flourished on his brow,
And he comes crowned with olive branches now.
Receive him! Oh, receive him as his friends;
Embrace the blessings which he recommends;
Such quiet as your foes shall ne'er destroy;   35
Then shake off fears, and clap your hands for joy.

---

30. *victories*] the exploits of the Duke of York as Lord High Admiral in
the Second Dutch War (1665–67). He resigned his offices after the Test
Act (March 1673).

The Orphan

or

The Unhappy Marriage

ACT I

Enter Paulino *and* Ernesto.

PAULINO.

    'Tis strange, Ernesto, this severity
    Should still reign pow'rful in Acasto's mind,
    To hate the Court where he was bred and lived,
    All honors heaped on him that pow'r could give.

ERNESTO.

    'Tis true. He came thither a private gentleman,   5
    But young and brave, and of a family
    Ancient and noble as the Empire holds.
    The honors he has gained are justly his;
    He purchased them in war. Thrice has he led
    An army against the rebels, and as often   10
    Returned with victory. The world has not
    A truer soldier, or a better subject.

PAULINO.

    It was his virtue that first made me serve him;
    He is the best of masters as of friends.
    I know he has lately been invited thither;   15

1–80. *Cut from performance after the*   3. he was] he/Was *Q1–4, W1*.
première (Gildon).

0.1] "Act I. Scene, a garden" (Bell). See Appendix B.

7. *Empire*] the loose federation of the different princes of Germany and
Central Europe under an emperor who in theory was elected by seven
electors, of whom the King of Bohemia was one. In practice the title was
hereditary in the House of Habsburg.

15. *thither*] to Court.

9

Yet still he keeps his stubborn purpose, cries
He's old, and willingly would be at rest:
I doubt there's deep resentment in his mind,
For the late slight his honor suffered there.

ERNESTO.

Has he not reason? When for what he had borne,   20
Long, hard, and faithful toil, he might have claimed
Places in honor and employment high,
A huffing, shining, flatt'ring, cringing coward,
A canker-worm of peace, was raised above him.

PAULINO.

Yet still he holds just value for the king,   25
Nor ever names him but with highest reverence.
'Tis noble that—

ERNESTO.

Oh, I have heard him, wanton in his praise,
Speak things of him might charm the ears of envy.

PAULINO.

Oh, may he live till Nature's self grow old,   30
And from her womb no more can bless the earth!
For when he dies, farewell all honor, bounty,
All generous encouragement of arts;
For charity herself becomes a widow.

ERNESTO.

No, he has two sons that were ordained to be   35
As well his virtue's, as his fortune's heirs.

PAULINO.

They're both of nature mild and full of sweetness.
They came twins from the womb, and still they live
As they would go twins too, to the grave.
Neither has anything he calls his own,   40
But of each other's joys as griefs partaking;
So very honestly, so well they love,
As they were only for each other born.

---

38. *twins*] Later Castalio is consistently referred to as the elder of the
two. Betterton (Castalio) was conspicuously older than Joseph Williams
(Polydore), who seems to have inherited the part from his master, Henry
Harris, Betterton's coeval.
42. *honestly*] sincerely, without fraud or falsehood.

ERNESTO.

Never was parent in an offspring happier.
He has a daughter too, whose blooming age   45
Promises goodness equal to her beauty.

PAULINO.

And as there is a friendship 'twixt the brethren,
So has her infant nature chosen, too,
A faithful partner of her thoughts and wishes,
And kind companion of her harmless pleasures.   50

ERNESTO.

You mean the beauteous orphan, fair Monimia?

PAULINO.

The same. The daughter of the brave Chamont.
He was our lord's companion in the wars,
Where such a wonderous friendship grew between 'em
As only death could end. Chamont's estate   55
Was ruined in our late and civil discords;
Therefore, unable to advance her fortune,
He left this daughter to our master's care;
To such a care as she scarce lost a father.

ERNESTO.

Her brother to the emperor's wars went early   60
To seek a fortune or a noble fate;
Whence he, with honor, is expected back,
And mighty marks of that great prince's favor.

PAULINO.

Our master never would permit his sons
To launch for fortune in th'uncertain world;   65
But warns to avoid both courts and camps,
Where dilatory fortune plays the jilt
With the brave, noble, honest, gallant man,
To throw herself away on fools and knaves.

66. warns] *Q1–4, W1;* warns 'em
Ghosh.

---

48. *infant*] in Common Law, not yet eighteen years of age.
    60. *emperor's wars*] Between 1672 and 1681, wars were waged by England, France, and Holland; by Poland, Russia, and Turkey; and by Sweden, Brandenburg, and Denmark.
    63. *prince*] From 1658 to 1705, the emperor was Leopold I.
    66. *courts and camps*] the best schools of heroic love and honor, according to Sir William D'Avenant (Preface to *Gondibert*, 1652).

ERNESTO.

> They both have forward, gen'rous, active spirits.   70
> 'Tis daily their petition to their father
> To send them forth where glory's to be gotten;
> They cry they're weary of their lazy home,
> Restless to do some thing that fame may talk of.
> Today they chased the boar, and near this time   75
> Should be returned.

PAULINO.   Oh, that's a royal sport!

> We yet may see the old man in a morning,
> Lusty as health, come ruddy to the field
> And there pursue the chase as if he meant
> To o'ertake time and bring back youth again.   80

Exeunt Ernesto *and* Paulino.

Enter Castalio, Polydore, *and* Page.

CASTALIO.

> Polydore! our sport
> Has been today much better for the danger.
> When on the brink the foaming boar I met,
> And in his side thought to have lodged my spear,
> The desperate savage rushed within my force,   85
> And bore me headlong with him down the rock.

POLYDORE.

> But then—

CASTALIO.

> Ay, then, my brother, my friend Polydore,
> Like Perseus mounted on his winged steed,
> Came on, and down the dang'rous precipice leapt   90
> To save Castalio. 'Twas a god-like act.

POLYDORE.

> But when I came, I found you conqueror.
> Oh, my heart danced to see your danger past!

---

76. *royal sport*] Until boars became extinct in England under Henry II, the sport was reserved for royalty. Boars, as distinguished from wild pigs, were still plentiful in Germany.

85. *within my force*] "within the range of his attack or defence" (*OED*); at such close range that the boar spear was unmanageable.

89. *Perseus*] Bellerophon rode the winged horse Pegasus; Perseus wore the winged sandals of Hermes. The confusion was fairly common.

The heat and fury of the chase was cooled,
And I had nothing in my mind but joy.   95

CASTALIO.

So, Polydore, methinks we might in war
Rush on together; thou shouldst be my guard,
And I'd be thine; what is't could hurt us then?
Now half the youth of Europe are in arms,
How fulsome must it be to stay behind,   100
And die of rank diseases here at home?

POLYDORE.

No, let me purchase in my youth renown,
To make me loved and valued when I'm old.
I would be busy in the world and learn—
Not, like a coarse and useless dunghill weed,   105
Fixed to one spot and rot just as I grew.

CASTALIO.

Our father
Has ta'en himself a surfeit of the world,
And cries it is not safe that we should taste it.
I own I have duty very pow'rful in me;   110
And though I'd hazard all to raise my name,
Yet he's so tender and so good a father,
I could not do a thing to cross his will.

POLYDORE.

Castalio, I have doubts within my heart
Which you, and only you, can satisfy.   115
Will you be free and candid to your friend?

CASTALIO.

Have I a thought my Polydore should not know?
What can this mean?   Nay, I'll conjure you too,
By all the strictest bonds of faithful friendship,
To show your heart as naked in this point,   120
As you would purge you of your sins to Heaven.

CASTALIO.

I will.

---

98. And I'd] *Q1;* And I *Q2–3; W1.*

---

113. *cross his will*] The remark brings Monimia to Polydore's mind,
suggesting that any entanglement with her might likewise "cross his will."

POLYDORE.

    And should I chance to touch it nearly, bear it
    With all the suff'rance of a tender friend.

CASTALIO.

    As calmly as the wounded patient bears   125
    The artist's hand that ministers his cure.

POLYDORE.

    That's kindly said. You know our father's ward
    The fair Monimia. Is your heart at peace?
    Is it so guarded that you could not love her?

CASTALIO.

    Suppose I should.

POLYDORE.   Suppose you should not, brother.   130

CASTALIO.

    You'd say I must not.

POLYDORE.   That would sound too roughly
    'Twixt friends and brothers, as we two are.

CASTALIO.

    Is love a fault?

POLYDORE.   In one of us it may be.
    What if I love her?

CASTALIO.   Then I must inform you,
    I loved her first and cannot quit the claim,   135
    But will preserve the birthright of my passion.

POLYDORE.

    You will!

CASTALIO.   I will.

POLYDORE.   No more, I've done.

CASTALIO.   Why not?

POLYDORE.

    I told you, I had done;
    But you, Castalio, would dispute it.

CASTALIO.   No!
    Not with my Polydore; though I must own   140
    My nature obstinate and void of suff'rance.
    Love reigns a very tyrant in my heart,
    Attended on his throne by all his guards
    Of furious wishes, fears, and nice suspicions.
    I could not bear a rival in my friendship,   145
    I am so much in love, and fond of thee.

POLYDORE.
   Yet you would break this friendship!
CASTALIO.   Not for crowns.
POLYDORE.
   But for a toy you would, a woman's toy!
   Unjust Castalio!
CASTALIO.   Prithee, where's my fault?
POLYDORE.
   You love Monimia.
CASTALIO.   Yes.
POLYDORE.   And you would kill me,   150
   If I'm your rival.
CASTALIO.   No. Sure we're such friends,
   So much one man, that our affections too
   Must be united and the same as we are.
POLYDORE.
   I dote upon Monimia.
CASTALIO.   Love her still;
   Win, and enjoy her.
POLYDORE.   Both of us cannot.
CASTALIO.   No matter   155
   Whose chance it proves, but let's not quarrel for't.
POLYDORE.
   You would not wed Monimia, would you?
CASTALIO.   Wed her!
   No. Were she all desire could wish, as fair
   As would the vainest of her sex be thought,
   With wealth beyond what woman's pride could waste,   160
   She should not cheat me of my freedom. Marry?
   When I am old and weary of the world,
   I may grow desperate
   And take a wife to mortify withal.
POLYDORE.
   It is an elder brother's duty so   165
   To propagate his family and name.
   You would not have yours die and buried with you?

151. we're] Q2–3; weare Q1.   160. woman's] Q2; woman Q1.

147. crowns] small gold coins, in 1688 worth five shillings. The German
Krone was worth more.
   148. toy] "dalliance" as well as plaything.

15

CASTALIO.

    Mere vanity, and silly dotage all.
    No, let me live at large, and when I die—

POLYDORE.

    Who shall possess th'estate you leave?

CASTALIO.   My friend,   170
    If he survives me, or if not, my king,
    Who may bestow't again on some brave man
    Whose honesty and services deserve one.

POLYDORE.

    'Tis kindly offered.

CASTALIO.   By yon Heaven, I love
    My Polydore beyond all worldly joys,   175
    And would not shock his quiet to be blessed
    With greater happiness than man e'er tasted.

POLYDORE.

    And by that Heaven eternally I swear
    To keep the kind Castalio in my heart.
    Whose shall Monimia be?

CASTALIO.   No matter whose.   180

POLYDORE.

    Were you not with her privately last night?

CASTALIO.

    I was, and should have met her here again,
    But th'opportunity shall now be thine;
    Myself will bring thee to the scene of love.
    But have a care, by friendship I conjure thee,   185
    That no false play be offered to thy brother.
    Urge all thy pow'rs to make thy passion prosper,
    But wrong not mine.

POLYDORE.   Heav'n blast me if I do.

CASTALIO.

    If't prove thy fortune, Polydore, to conquer
    (For thou hast all the arts of fine persuasion!),   190
    Trust me, and let me know thy love's success,
    That I may ever after stifle mine.

POLYDORE.

    Though she be dearer to my soul than rest
    To weary pilgrims, or to misers gold,
    To great men pow'r, or wealthy cities pride,   195

16

Rather than wrong Castalio I'd forget her.
For if ye pow'rs have happiness in store
When ye would shower down joys on Polydore,
In one great blessing all your bounty send,
That I may never lose so dear a friend.   200
        Exeunt Castalio *and* Polydore. *Manet* Page.

     Enter Monimia.

MONIMIA.
So soon returned from hunting? This fair day
Seems as if sent to invite the world abroad.
Passed not Castalio and Polydore this way?
PAGE.
Madam, just now.
MONIMIA [*aside*]. Sure, some ill fate's upon me.
Distrust and heaviness sits round my heart,   205
And apprehension shocks my timorous soul.
Why was I not lain in my peaceful grave
With my poor parents and at rest as they are?
Instead of that, I am wand'ring into cares.
Castalio! Oh, Castalio! Thou hast caught   210
My foolish heart; and like a tender child
That trusts his plaything to another hand,
I fear its harm, and fain would have it back.—
[*To the* Page.] Come near, Cordelio, I must chide you, sir.
PAGE.
Why, madam, have I done you any wrong?   215
MONIMIA.
I never see you now; you have been kinder;
Sat by my bed, and sung me pretty songs.
Perhaps I've been ungrateful; here's money for you.
Will you oblige me? Shall I see you oft'ner?
PAGE.
Madam, indeed I'd serve you with my soul;   220
But in a morning when you call me to you,
As by your bed I stand and tell you stories,
I am ashamed to see your swelling breasts;
It makes me blush, they are so very white.

202. to invite] *Q2;* t'invite *Q1.*   220. indeed] *Q1; om. Q2–3, W1.*

MONIMIA.

    Oh, men, for flattery and deceit renowned!   225
    Thus, when y'are young, ye learn it all like him,
    Till as your years increase, that strengthens too,
    T'undo poor maids and make our ruin easy.
    Tell me, Cordelio, for thou hast oft heard
    Their friendly converse, and their bosom secrets,   230
    Sometimes at least, have they not talked of me?

PAGE.

    Oh, madam, very wickedly they have talked;
    But I'm afraid to name it, for they say
    Boys must be whipped that tell their master's secrets.

MONIMIA.

    Fear not, Cordelio, it shall ne'er be known,   235
    For I'll preserve the secret as 'twere mine;
    Polydore cannot be so kind as I.
    I'll furnish thee for all thy harmless sports
    With pretty toys, and thou shalt be my page.

PAGE.

    And truly, madam, I had rather be so.   240
    Methinks you love me better than my lord,
    For he was never half so kind as you are.
    What must I do?

MONIMIA.   Inform me how th'hast heard
    Castalio and his brother use my name.

PAGE.

    With all the tenderness of love,   245
    You were the subject of their last discourse.
    At first I thought it would have fatal proved;
    But as the one grew hot the other cooled,
    And yielded to the frailty of his friend.
    At last, after much struggling 'twas resolv'd—   250

MONIMIA.

    What, good Cordelio?

PAGE.   Not to quarrel for you.

MONIMIA.

    I would not have 'em, by my dearest hopes,
    I would not be the argument of strife.

---

247. *fatal proved*] Cf. l. 150. "And you would kill me/ If I'm your rival."

[*Aside.*] But surely my Castalio won't forsake me,
And make a mockery of my easy love.   255
[*To the* Page.] Went they together?
PAGE.   Yes, to seek you, madam.
Castalio promised Polydore to bring him
Where he alone might meet you,
And fairly try the fortune of his wishes.
MONIMIA [*aside*].
Am I then grown so cheap, just to be made   260
A common stake, a prize for love in jest?
[*To the* Page.]   Was not Castalio very loth to yield it,
Or was it Polydore's unruly passion
That heightened the debate?
PAGE.   The fault was Polydore's.
Castalio played with love and smiling showed   265
The pleasure, not the pangs of his desire.
He said no woman's smiles should buy his freedom;
And marriage is a mortifying thing.
MONIMIA [*aside*].
Then am I ruined. If Castalio's false,
Where is there faith or honor to be found?   270
Ye gods, that guard the innocent and guide
The weak, protect and take me to your care.
Oh, but I love him. There's the rock will wrack me.
Why was I made with all my sex's softness,
Yet want the cunning to conceal its follies?   275
I'll see Castalio, tax him with his falsehoods;
Be a true woman, rail, protest my wrongs,
Resolve to hate him, and yet love him still.

Enter Castalio *and* Polydore.

He comes, the conqueror comes! Lie still, my heart,
And learn to bear thy injuries with scorn.   280
CASTALIO.
Madam, my brother begs he may have leave
To tell you something that concerns you nearly.
I leave you, as becomes me, and withdraw.
MONIMIA.
My Lord Castalio!
CASTALIO.   Madam!

MONIMIA.　　　　　　　　　Have you purposed
　　To abuse me palpably? What means this usage?　　285
　　Why am I left with Polydore alone?
CASTALIO.
　　He best can tell you. Business of importance
　　Calls me away; I must attend my father.
MONIMIA.
　　Will you then leave me thus?
CASTALIO.　　　　　　　　　But for a moment.
MONIMIA.
　　It has been otherwise; the time has been　　　290
　　When business might have stayed, and I been heard.
CASTALIO.
　　I could forever hear thee; but this time
　　Matters of such odd circumstances press me,
　　That I must go—
MONIMIA.
　　Then go; and if't be possible, forever.　　　　295
　　　　　　　　　　　　　　　　　Exit Castalio.
　　Well, my Lord Polydore, I guess your business,
　　And read the ill-natured purpose in your eyes.
POLYDORE.
　　If to desire you more than misers wealth,
　　Or dying men an hour of added life;
　　If softest wishes, and a heart more true　　　300
　　Than ever suffered yet for love disdained,
　　Speak an ill nature, you accuse me justly.
MONIMIA.
　　Talk not of love, my lord, I must not hear it.
POLYDORE.
　　Who can behold such beauty, and be silent?
　　Desire first taught us words. Man, when created,　　305
　　At first alone long wandered up and down,
　　Forlorn and silent as his vassal beasts;
　　But when a heaven-born maid, like you, appeared,
　　Strange pleasures filled his eyes, and fired his heart,
　　Unloosed his tongue, and his first talk was love.　　310
MONIMIA.
　　The first created pair, indeed, were blest;

---

298. *than misers wealth*] i.e., than misers desire wealth.

They were the only objects of each other;
Therefore he courted her, and her alone.
But in this peopled world of beauty, where
There's roving room, where you may court, and ruin   315
A thousand more, why need you talk to me?

POLYDORE.

Oh, I could talk to thee forever; thus
Eternally admiring, fix and gaze
On those dear eyes, for every glance they send
Darts through my soul, and almost gives enjoyment.   320

MONIMIA.

How can you labor thus for my undoing?
I must confess, indeed, I owe you more
Than I can hope to think to pay.
There always was a friendship 'twixt our families;
And therefore when my tender parents died,   325
Whose ruined fortunes, too, expired with them,
Your father's pity, and his bounty, took me,
A poor and helpless orphan to his care.

POLYDORE.

'Twas Heav'n ordained it so, to make me happy.
Hence with this peevish virtue, 'tis a cheat;   330
And those who taught it first were hypocrites.
Come, those soft tender limbs were made for yielding.

MONIMIA.

Here on my knees, by Heaven's blest pow'r I swear, *Kneels.*
If you persist, I never henceforth will see you;
But rather wander through the world a beggar,   335
And live on sordid scraps at proud men's doors;
For though to fortune lost, I'll still inherit
My mother's virtues and my father's honor.

POLYDORE.

Intolerable vanity! your sex
Was never in the right; y'are always false   340
Or silly. Even your dresses are not more
Fantastic then your appetites. You think
Of nothing twice. Opinion you have none.
Today y'are nice, to-morrow not so free;

---

344. *nice*] here meaning tender or wanton, rather than difficult to
please, fastidious, precise.

Now smile, then frown; now sorrowful, then glad;   345
Now pleased, now not; and all you know not why.
Virtue you affect, inconstancy's your practice;
And when your loose desires once get dominion,
No hungry churl feeds coarser at a feast;
Every rank fool goes down—

MONIMIA.   Indeed, my lord,   350
I own my sex's follies; I have 'em all,
And to avoid its faults must fly from you.
Therefore, believe me: could you raise me high
As most fantastic woman's wish could reach,
And lay all Nature's riches at my feet,   355
I'd rather run a savage in the woods
Amongst brute beasts, grow wrinkled and deformed
As wildness and most rude neglect could make me,
So I might still enjoy my honor safe
From the destroying wiles of faithless man.   360

Exit Monimia.

POLYDORE [_solus_].

Who'd be that sordid foolish thing called man,
To cringe thus, fawn, and flatter for a pleasure,
Which beasts enjoy so very much above him?
The lusty bull ranges through all the field,
And from the herd singling his female out,   365
Enjoys her, and abandons her at will.
It shall be so. I'll yet possess my love,
Wait on, and watch her loose unguarded hours;
Then, when her roving thoughts have been abroad
And brought in wanton wishes to her heart—   370
I'th' very minute when her virtue nods,
I'll rush upon her in a storm of love,
Bear down her guard of honor all before me,
Surfeit on joys till even desire grows sick:
Then by long absence, liberty regain   375
And quite forget the pleasure and the pain.

Exeunt Polydore _and_ Page.

349. at a feast] _Q3, W1, Ghosh;_ at feast _Q1–2._

22

ACT II

Enter Acasto, Castalio, Polydore, *Attendants.*

ACASTO.
Today has been a day of glorious sport.
When you, Castalio, and your brother left me,
Forth from the thickets rushed another boar,
So large he seemed the tyrant of the woods;
With all his dreadful bristles raised up high,   5
They seemed a grove of spears upon his back;
Foaming he came at me (where I was posted
Best to observe which way he'd lead the chase),
Whetting his huge long tusks, and gaping wide
As if he already had me for his prey;   10
Till brandishing my well poised javelin high,
With this cold executing arm I struck
The ugly brindled monster to the heart.
CASTALIO.
The actions of your life were always wondrous.
ACASTO.
No flattery, boy! An honest man can't live by't;   15
It is a little sneaking art, which knaves
Use to cajole and soften fools withal.
If thou has flatt'ry in thy nature, out with't,
Or send it to a court, for there 'twill thrive.
POLYDORE.
Why there?
ACASTO.   'Tis next to money current there,   20
To be seen daily in as many forms
As there are sorts of vanities and men.
The superstitious statesman has his sneer
To smooth a poor man off with that can't bribe him.

---

12. cold] *Q1–4, W1;* bold *Ghosh.*   23. superstitious] *Q1–4, W1;*
superilious *Ghosh.*

0.1. "Act II. Scene, a saloon" (Bell).

12. *cold*] without excitement; with cold deliberation.

23. *superstitious*] in the Latin sense of "standing upon or over"; therefore, excessively self-important, as in "superstitious conceit of his own
merit" (*OED,* 1638).

The grave dull fellow of small business soothes   25
The humorist, and will needs admire his wit.
Who without spleen could see a hot-brained atheist
Thanking a surly Doctor for his sermon;
Or a grave councillor meet a smooth young lord,
Squeeze him by the hand, and praise his good complex-
    ion?   30
POLYDORE.
Courts are the places where best manners flourish,
Where the deserving ought to rise, and fools
Make show. Why should I vex and chafe my spleen
To see a gawdy coxcomb shine, when I
Have seen enough to soothe him in his follies,   35
And ride him to advantage as I please?
ACASTO.
Who merit ought indeed to rise i'th' world;
But no wise man that's honest should expect.
What man of sense would rack his generous mind
To practice all the base formalities   40
And forms of business, force a grave starched face
When he's a very libertine in's heart?
Seem not to know this or that man in public,
When privately, perhaps, they meet together
And lay the scene of some brave fellow's ruin?   45
Such things are done—
CASTALIO.   Your lordship's wrongs have been
So great that you with justice may complain;
But suffer us, whose younger minds ne'er felt
Fortune's deceits, to court her as she's fair.
Were she a common mistress, kind to all,   50
Her worth would cease, and half the world grow idle.
ACASTO.
Go to, y'are fools, and know me not; I've learned
Long since to bear, revenge, or scorn my wrongs
According to the value of the doer.
You both would fain be great; and to that end   55
Desire to do things worthy your ambition.

---

26. *humorist*] a fanciful, capricious wag; a crotchety person.
27. *spleen*] indignation. In l. 33, the seat of morose feelings.

Go to the camp, preferment's noblest mart,
Where honor ought to have the fairest play, you'll find
Corruption, envy, discontent, and faction
Almost in every band. How many men   60
Have spent their blood in their dear country's service,
Yet now pine under want; while selfish slaves,
That ev'n would cut their throats whom now they fawn on,
Like deadly locusts eat the honey up
Which those industrious bees so hardly toiled for?   65

CASTALIO.
These precepts suit not with my active mind.
Methinks I would be busy.

POLYDORE.   So would I;
Not loiter out my life at home, and know
No farther than one prospect gives me leave.

ACASTO.
Busy your minds then; study arts and men;   70
Learn how to value merits though in rags,
And scorn a proud ill-mannered knave in office.

Enter Serina, Monimia, *and Maid.*

SERINA.
My lord, my father!

ACASTO.   Blessings on my child.
My little cherub, what hast thou to ask me?

SERINA.
I bring you, sir, most glad and welcome news: 75
The young Chamont, whom you've so often wished for,
Is just arrived and ent'ring.

ACASTO.   By my soul,
And all my honors, he's most dearly welcome.
Let me receive him like his father's friend.

Enter Chamont.

Welcome, thou relic of the best loved man;   80
Welcome from all the turmoils, and the hazards
Of certain danger and uncertain fortune;
Welcome as happy tidings after fears.

---

63. *throats whom*] cut the throats of those (they fawn on).

CHAMONT.
> Words would but wrong the gratitude I owe you.
> Should I begin to speak, my soul's so full   85
> That I should talk of nothing else all day.

MONIMIA.
> My brother!

CHAMONT.   Oh, my sister! Let me hold thee
> Long in my arms; I've not beheld thy face
> These many days; by night I've often seen thee
> In gentle dreams, and satisfied my soul   90
> With fancied joy, till morning cares awaked me.
> [*To* Serina.] Another sister? Sure it must be so;
> Though I remember well I had but one.
> But I feel something in my heart that prompts
> And tells me she has claim and interest there.   95

ACASTO.
> Young soldier, you've not only studied war;
> Courtship I see has been your practice too,
> And may not prove unwelcome to my daughter.

CHAMONT.
> Is she your daughter? Then my heart told true!
> And I'm at least her brother by adoption,   100
> For you have made yourself to me a father
> And by that patent I have leave to love her.

SERINA [*aside to* Monimia].
> Monimia, thou hast told me men are false,
> Will flatter, feign and make an art of love.
> Is Chamont so? No, sure he's more than man,   105
> Something that's near divine, and truth dwells in him.

ACASTO.
> Thus happy, who would envy pompous pow'r,
> The luxury of courts, or wealth of cities?
> Let there be joy through all the house this day!
> In every room let plenty flow at large: 110
> It is the birthday of my Royal Master.
> You have not visited the court, Chamont,
> Since your return?

CHAMONT.   I have no business there.
> I have not slavish temperance enough
> T'attend a favorite's heels, and watch his smiles,   115

Bear an ill office done me to my face,
And thank the lord that wronged me for his favor.

ACASTO *(to his sons).*
This you could do.

CASTALIO.   I'd serve my prince.

ACASTO.   Who'd serve him?

CASTALIO.
I would, my lord.

POLYDORE.   And I, both would.

ACASTO.   Away.
He needs not any servants such as you!   120
Serve him! He merits more than man can do.
He is so good, praise cannot speak his worth;
So merciful, sure he ne'er slept in wrath;
So just, that were he but a private man,
He could not do a wrong. How would you serve him?   125

CASTALIO.
I'd serve him with my fortune here at home,
And serve him with my person in his wars.
Watch for him, fight for him, bleed for him—

POLYDORE.   Die for him,
As every true-born loyal subject ought.

ACASTO.
Let me embrace ye both. Now by the souls   130
Of my brave ancestors, I'm truly happy!
For this be ever blest my marriage day;
Blest be your mother's memory that bore you;
And doubly blest be that auspicious hour
That gave the birth. Yes, my aspiring boys,   135
Ye shall have business when your master wants you;
You cannot serve a nobler. I have served him;
In this old body yet the marks remain
Of many wounds. I've with this tongue proclaimed
His right, even in the face of rank rebellion;   140
And when a foul-mouthed traitor once profaned
His sacred name, with my good saber drawn,
Ev'n at the head of all his giddy rout

135. gave the] *Q1–4;* gave ye *W1,*
Ghosh.

I rushed, and clove the rebel to the chine.

Enter Servant.

SERVANT.
 My lord, the expected guests are just arrived.   145
ACASTO [*to* Castalio *and* Polydore].
 Go you, and give 'em welcome and reception.
                    Exeunt all but Acasto, Chamont, *and* Monimia.
CHAMONT.
 My lord, I stand in need of your assistance
 In something that concerns my peace and honor.
ACASTO.
 Spoke like the son of that brave man I loved;
 So freely friendly we conversed together.   150
 Whate'er it be, with confidence impart it;
 Thou shalt command my fortune and my sword.
CHAMONT.
 I dare not doubt your friendship nor your justice.
 Your bounty shown to what I hold most dear,
 My orphan sister, must not be forgotten.   155
ACASTO.
 Prithee, no more of that, it grates my nature.
CHAMONT.
 When our dear parents died, they died together;
 One fate surprised 'em, and one grave received 'em.
 My father, with his dying breath, bequeathed
 Her to my love. My mother, as she lay   160
 Languishing by him, called me to her side,
 Took me in her fainting arms, wept, and embraced me,
 Then pressed me close; and as she observed my tears,
 Kissed 'em away. Said she, "Chamont, my son,
 By this and all the love I ever showed thee,   165
 Be careful of Monimia; watch her youth;
 Let not her wants betray her to dishonor.
 Perhaps kind Heav'n may raise some friend—" Then
     sighed,

---

168. Then sigh'd] *W1, Ghosh; itali-*   S.D. Q1–4.
cized and set off in right margin as

---

144. *chine*] backbone; cervical vertebrae.

Kissed me again, so blessed us, and expired—
Pardon my grief.
ACASTO.   It speaks an honest nature.   170
CHAMONT.
The friend Heav'n raised was you. You took her up,
An infant to the desert world exposed,
And proved another parent.
ACASTO.   I've not wronged her.
CHAMONT.
Far be it from my fears.
ACASTO.   Then why this argument?
CHAMONT.
My lord, my nature's jealous, and you'll bear it.   175
ACASTO.
Go on.
CHAMONT. Great spirits bear misfortunes hardly;
Good offices claim gratitude, and pride,
Where pow'r is wanting, will usurp a little;
May make us (rather than be thought behindhand)
Pay over-price.
ACASTO   I cannot guess your drift.   180
Distrust you me?
CHAMONT.   No, but I fear her weakness
May make her pay a debt at any rate;
And to deal freely with your lordship's goodness,
I've heard a story lately much disturbs me.
ACASTO.
Then first charge her; and if th'offense be found   185
Within my reach, though it should touch my nature
In my own offspring, by the dear remembrance
Of thy brave father, whom my heart rejoiced in,
I'd prosecute it with severest vengeance.
                                                    Exit Acasto.
CHAMONT.
I thank you from my soul.
MONIMIA.   Alas, my brother!   190
What have I done? And why do you abuse me?
My heart quakes in me; in your settled face

---

175. *jealous*] suspicious; intolerant of any defection or deviation from the strictest honor.

And clouded brow methinks I see my fate.
You will not kill me!
CHAMONT.   Prithee, why dost talk so?
MONIMIA.

Look kindly on me then; I cannot bear   195
Severity; it daunts, and does amaze me.
My heart's so tender, should you charge me roughly,
I should but weep, and answer you with sobbing;
But use me gently like a loving brother,
And search through all the secrets of my soul.   200
CHAMONT.

Fear nothing. I will show myself a brother,
A tender, honest and a loving brother.
Y'ave not forgot our father!
MONIMIA.   I shall never.
CHAMONT.

Then you'll remember too, he was a man
That lived up to the standard of his honor,   205
And prized that jewel more than mines of wealth.
He'd not have done a shameful thing but once;
Though kept in darkness from the world, and hidden,
He could not have forgiven it to himself.
This was the only portion that he left us;   210
And I more glory in't than if possessed
Of all that ever fortune threw on fools.
'Twas a large trust, and must be managed nicely.
Now, if by any chance, Monimia,
You have soiled this gem and taken from its value,   215
How will y'account with me?
MONIMIA.   I challenge envy,
Malice, and all the practices of hell,
To censure all the actions of my past
Unhappy life, and taint me if they can!
CHAMONT.

I'll tell thee then. Three nights ago, as I   220
Lay musing in my bed, all darkness round me,
A sudden damp struck to my heart; cold sweat
Dewed all my face, and trembling seized my limbs;
My bed shook under me, the curtains started,
And to my tortured fancy there appeared   225

The form of thee thus beauteous as thou art,
Thy garments flowing loose, and in each hand
A wanton lover, which by turns caressed thee
With all the freedom of unbounded pleasure.
I snatched my sword, and in the very moment   230
Darted it at the phantom—straight it left me;
Then rose and called for lights, when, oh, dire omen!
I found my weapon had the arras pierced
Just where that famous tale was interwoven,
How th'unhappy Theban slew his father.   235

MONIMIA.
And for this cause my virtue is suspected!
Because in dreams your fancy has been ridden,
I must be tortured waking!

CHAMONT.   Have a care;
Labor not to be justified too fast.
Hear all, and then let justice hold the scale.   240
What followed was the riddle that confounds me:
Through a close lane, as I pursued my journey
And meditated on the last night's vision,
I spied a wrinkled hag, with age grown double,
Picking dry sticks and mumbling to herself.   245
Her eyes with scalding rheum were galled and red;
Cold palsy shook her head; her hands seemed withered;
And on her crooked shoulders had she wrapped
The tattered remnant of an old stripped hanging,
Which served to keep her carcass from the cold,   250
So there was nothing of a piece about her.
Her lower weeds were all o'er coarsely patched
With diff'rent colored rags, black, red, white, yellow,
And seemed to speak variety of wretchedness.

---

249. stripped]   script   *Q1–2*
(?striped).

---

235. *Theban*] Oedipus, who unwittingly killed his father Laius on the
road from Corinth to Thebes. The play *Oedipus* by Dryden and Lee had
been performed at Dorset Garden (September 1678) for "10 Days together."

244. *hag*] later called a *witch*. Chamont's "rant," like his dream, and
later Acasto's, supplies the conventional supernatural element expected in
a heroic play.

I asked of her my way, which she informed me;   255
Then craved my charity, and bade me hasten
To save a sister: at that word I started.

MONIMIA.

The common cheat of beggars every day!
They flock about our doors, pretend to gifts
Of prophecy, and telling fools their fortunes.   260

CHAMONT.

Oh, but she told me such a tale, Monimia,
As in it bore great circumstance of truth.
Castalio and Polydore, my sister—

MONIMIA.   Hah!

CHAMONT.

What, altered? Does your courage fail you?
Now, by my father's soul, the witch was honest.   265
Answer me, if thou has not lost to them
Thy honor at a sordid game.

MONIMIA.   I will.

I must. So hardly my misfortune loads me,
That both have offered me their love's most true—

CHAMONT.

And 'tis as true, too, they have both undone thee.   270

MONIMIA.

Though they both with earnest vows
Have pressed my heart, if e'er in thought I yielded
To any but Castalio—

CHAMONT.   But Castalio!

MONIMIA.

Still will you cross the line of my discourse!
Yes, I confess that he has won my soul   275
By generous love and honorable vows,
Which he this day appointed to complete,
And make himself by holy marriage mine.

CHAMONT.

Art thou then spotless? Hast thou still preserved
Thy virtue white without a blot untainted?   280

MONIMIA.

When I'm unchaste, may Heaven reject my prayers!
Or more, to make me wretched, may you know it!

CHAMONT.

    Oh then, Monimia, art thou dearer to me
    Than all the comforts ever yet blessed man.
    And let not marriage bait thee to thy ruin: 285
    Trust not a man. We are by nature false,
    Dissembling, subtle, cruel, and unconstant.
    When a man talks of love, with caution trust him;
    But if he swears, he'll certainly deceive thee.
    I charge thee, let no more Castalio soothe thee.   290
    Avoid it, as thou wouldst preserve the peace
    Of a poor brother, to whose soul th'art precious.

MONIMIA.

    I will.

CHAMONT.

    Appear as cold when next you meet, as great ones
    When merit begs; then shalt thou see how soon   295
    His heart will cool and all his pains grow easy.

                                             Exit Chamont.

MONIMIA.

    Yes, I will try him, torture him severely;
    For, oh, Castalio, thou too much has wronged me
    In leaving me to Polydore's ill usage.
    He comes; and now for once, oh love, stand neuter   300
    Whilst a hard part's performed. For I must tempt,
    Wound his soft nature, though my own heart aches for't.

                                          Exit Monimia.

                Enter Castalio.

CASTALIO.

    Monimia, Monimia— she's gone,
    And seemed to part with anger in her eyes.
    I am a fool, and she has found my weakness.   305
    She uses me already like a slave
    Fast bound in chains, to be chastised at will.
    'Twas not well done to trifle with my brother;
    I might have trusted him with all the secret,

---

    287. *And . . . ruin*] Chamont fears a secret marriage where there are no
witnesses, and especially one contracted without parental approval. The
fate of Lady Catherine Grey (1560), of Mrs. Davenport, the actress (1662),
and currently of William Wycherley (1680), are cases in point.

Opened my silly heart and shown it bare.   310
But then he loves her too; but not like me.
I am a doting honest slave, designed
For bondage, marriage bonds—which I've sworn
To wear. It is the only thing I e'er
Hid from his knowledge; and he'll sure forgive   315
The first transgression of a wretched friend
Betrayed to love and all its little follies.

Enter Polydore *and Page at the door.*

POLYDORE.
Here place yourself, and watch my brother throughly.
If he should chance to meet Monimia, make
Just observation of each word and action.   320
Pass not one circumstance without remark.
Sir, 'tis your office. Do't and bring me word.

                                 Exit Polydore.

Enter Monimia.

CASTALIO.
Monimia, my angel, 'twas not kind
To leave me like a turtle here alone,
To droop and mourn the absence of my mate.   325
When thou art from me every place is desert,
And I, methinks, am savage and forlorn.
Thy presence only 'tis can make me blest,
Heal my unquiet mind, and tune my soul.
MONIMIA.
Oh, the bewitching tongues of faithless men!   330
'Tis thus the false hyena makes her moan,
To draw the pitying traveller to her den;
Your sex are so; such false dissemblers all.
With sighs and plaints y'entice poor women's hearts,
And all that pity you are made your prey.   335

---

318. *throughly*] thoroughly, closely.
324. *turtle*] turtle-dove.
326. *thou*] the intimate form of affection, in contrast to the formal *you*,
indicative here of wounded feelings and outrage; elsewhere, used either
in contempt, or to an inferior and servant.

CASTALIO.

    What means my love? Oh, how have I deserved
    This language from the sovereign of my joys?
    Stop, stop those tears, Monimia, for they fall
    Like baneful dew from a distempered sky:
    I feel 'em chill me to the very heart.   340

MONIMIA.

    Oh, you are false, Castalio, most forlorn!
    Attempt no farther to delude my faith;
    My heart is fixed, and you shall shake't no more.

CASTALIO.

    Who told you so? What hell-bred villain durst
    Profane the sacred business of my love?   345

MONIMIA.

    Your brother, knowing on what terms I'm here,
    Th'unhappy object of your father's charity,
    Licentiously discoursed to me of love,
    And durst affront me with his brutal passion.

CASTALIO.

    'Tis I have been to blame, and only I,   350
    False to my brother and unjust to thee.
    For, oh, he loves thee too, and this day owned it;
    Taxed me with mine, and claimed a right above me.

MONIMIA.

    And was your love so very tame to shrink,
    Or rather than lose him, abandon me?   355

CASTALIO.

    I, knowing him precipitate and rash,
    To calm his heat and to conceal my happiness,
    Seemed to comply with his unruly will;
    Talked as he talked, and granted all he asked,
    Lest he in rage might have our loves betrayed,   360
    And I forever had Monimia lost.

MONIMIA.

    Could you then? Did you? Can you own it too?
    'Twas poorly done, unworthy of yourself,
    And I can never think you meant me fair.

341. forlorn] *Q1–3;* forsworn
Ghosh.

---

341. *forlorn*] lost, in the sense of morally lost; depraved (*OED*).

CASTALIO.

Is this Monimia? Surely no! Till now   365
I ever thought her dove-like, soft, and kind.
Who trusts his heart with woman's surely lost!
You were made fair on purpose to undo us,
Whilst greedily we snatch th'alluring bait,
And ne'er distrust the poison that it hides.   370

MONIMIA.

When love ill placed would find a means to break—

CASTALIO.

It never wants pretenses nor excuse.

MONIMIA.

Man therefore was a lordlike creature made,
Rough as the winds, and as inconstant too;
A lofty aspect given him for command,   375
Easily softened, when he would betray;
Like conquering tyrants, you our breasts invade,
Where you are pleased to forage for a while;
But soon you find new conquests out, and leave
The ravaged province ruinate and waste.   380
If so, Castalio, you have served my heart,
I find that desolation's settled there,
And I shall ne'er recover peace again.

CASTALIO.

Who can hear this and bear an equal mind!
Since you will drive me from you, I must go;   385
But, oh, Monimia, when th'hast banished me,
No creeping slave, though tractable and dull
As artful woman for her ends would choose,
Shall ever dote as I have done; for, oh,
No tongue my pleasure nor my pain can tell: 390
'Tis Heav'n to have thee, and without thee Hell.

MONIMIA.

Castalio, stay! We must not part. I find
My rage ebbs out, and love flows in apace.
These little quarrels love must needs forgive,
They rouse up drowsy thoughts, and wake the soul. 395

---

387. *creeping slave*] The manliness and restraint of Betterton, who created the role, would serve as a corrective to Castalio's too-lush sentiments.

Oh, charm me with the music of thy tongue;
I'm ne'er so blest, as when I hear thy vows,
And listen to the language of thy heart.

CASTALIO.

   Where am I? Surely Paradise is round me!
   Sweets planted by the hand of Heaven grow here,   400
   And every sense is full of thy perfection.
   To hear thee speak might calm a madman's frenzy,
   Till by attention he forgot his sorrows;
   But to behold thy eyes, th'amazing beauties,
   Might make him rage again with love, as I do.   405
   To touch thee's Heav'n, but to enjoy thee, oh!
   Thou Nature's whole perfection in one piece!
      Sure framing thee Heav'n took unusual care;
      As its own beauty it designed thee fair;
      And formed thee by the best-loved Angel there.   410

Exeunt [Castalio *and* Monimia *at one door, and the Page at
the other*].

ACT III

Enter Polydore, *and* Page.

POLYDORE.

Were they so kind? Express it to me all
In words may make me think I saw it too.

PAGE.

At first I thought they had been mortal foes;
Monimia raged, Castalio grew disturbed;
Each thought the other wronged, yet both so haughty   5
They scorned submission; though love all the while
The rebel played, and scarce could be contained.

POLYDORE.

But what succeeded?

PAGE.   Oh, 'twas wondrous pretty!

For of a sudden all the storm was past;
A gentle calm of love succeeded in;   10
Monimia sighed and blushed, Castalio swore,
As you, my lord, I well remember, did
To my young sister in the orange grove,
When I was first preferred to be your page.

POLYDORE [*aside*].

Happy Castalio! Now by my great soul,   15
M'ambitious soul, that languishes to glory,
I'll have her yet, by my best hopes I will.
She shall be mine in spite of all her arts.
But for Castalio why was I refused?
Has he supplanted me by some foul play?   20
Traduced my honor? Death! He durst not do't.
It must be so: we parted and he met her,
Half to compliance brought by me; surprised
Her sinking virtue till she yielded quite.
So poachers basely pick up tired game,   25
Whilst the fair hunter's cheated of his prey.
Boy!

0.1. "Act III. Scene, a garden" (Bell).

16. *M'ambitious*] The elision is permitted because *my* was pronounced
very like *me*. See Otto L. Jiriczek's edition of *Alexander Gill's Logonomia
Anglica* (Strassburg, 1903), Index, s.v. "my."

PAGE.

   My lord.

POLYDORE.

   Go to your chamber and prepare your lute;
   Find out some song to please me, that describes   30
   Women's hypocrisies, their subtle wiles,
   Betraying smiles, feigned tears, inconstancies,
   Their painted outsides, and corrupted minds,
   The sum of all their follies and their falsehoods.

                                          [*Exit* Page.]

                    Enter Servant.

SERVANT.

   Oh, the unhappiest tidings tongue e'er told!   35

POLYDORE.

   The matter?

SERVANT.   Oh, your father, my good master!
   As with his guests he sat in mirth raised high,
   And chased the goblins round the joyful board,
   A sudden trembling seized on all his limbs;
   His eyes distorted grew, his visage pale;   40
   His speech forsook him; life itself seemed fled;
   And all his friends are waiting now about him.

              Enter Acasto *leaning on two.*

ACASTO.

   Support me, give me air, I'll yet recover.
   'Twas but a slip decaying nature made,
   For she grows weary near her journey's end.   45
   Where are my sons? Come near, my Polydore.
   Your brother—Where's Castalio?

SERVANT.   My lord,
   I've searched, as you commanded, all the house;
   He or Monimia are not to be found.

38. goblins] *Q1;* goblings *Q2–3;*
gobling *Q4, W1;* goblet *Bell; Ghosh.*

   38. *chased the goblins*] chased "blue devils" or depressing thoughts away.
Cf. Milton's "Goblin," Death (*Paradise Lost,* 2, 687). Overtones from
Paradise Lost recur at II. 400–402, and at 307–10 and 588–94 below.

ACASTO.

    Not to be found! Then where are all my friends?   50
    'Tis well.
    I hope they'll pardon an unhappy fault
    M'unmannerly infirmity has made.
    Death could not come in a more welcome hour,
    For I'm prepared to meet him, and methinks   55
    Would live and die with all my friends about me.

        Enter Castalio [*followed by* Monimia].

CASTALIO.

    Angels preserve my dearest father's life,
    Bless it with long and uninterrupted days!
    Oh, may he live till time itself decay,
    Till good men wish him dead—or I offend him.   60

ACASTO.

    Thank you, Castalio. Give me both your hands,
    And bear me up; I'd walk. So, now methinks
    I appear as great as Hercules himself,
    Supported by the pillars he had raised.

CASTALIO.

    My lord, your chaplain.

ACASTO.   Let the good man enter.   65

           [*Enter* Chaplain.]

CHAPLAIN.

    Heaven guard your lordship, and restore your health!

ACASTO.

    I have provided for thee, if I die.
    No fawning! 'Tis a scandal to thy office.
    My sons, as thus united, ever live;
    And for the estate, you'll find when I am dead   70
    I have divided it betwixt you both,
    Equally parted, as you shared my love;

66. S.P. CHAPLAIN] *Q3;* CASTALIO
Q1–2.

    63–64. *Hercules . . . pillars*] Acasto is perhaps thinking of Mount Atlas,
which supported Hercules when he bore the world on his shoulders,
rather than of the two mountains on either side of the Straits of Gibraltar,
said by Pliny and by Strabo to have been joined until Hercules separated
them and made an outlet for the Mediterranean into the Atlantic Ocean.

Only to sweet Monimia I've bequeathed
Ten thousand crowns, a little portion for her,
To wed her honorably as she's born.   75
Be not less friends because you're brothers; shun
The man that's singular: his mind's unsound,
His spleen o'erweights his brains. But above all,
Avoid the politic, the factious fool,
The busy, buzzing, talking, hardened knave,   80
The quaint, smooth rogue, that sins against his reason,
Calls saucy loud suspicion, public zeal,
And mutiny, the dictates of his spirit.
Be very careful how ye make new friends:
Men read not morals now; 'twas a custom—   85
But all are to their father's vices born,
And in their mother's ignorance are bred.
Let marriage be the last mad thing ye do,
For all the sins and follies of the past.
If you have children, never give them knowledge: 90
'Twill spoil their fortune; fools are all the fashion.
If y'ave religion, keep it to yourselves;
Atheists will else make use of toleration,
And laugh ye out on't. Never show religion
Except ye mean to pass for knaves of conscience,   95
And cheat believing fools that think ye honest.

[*Enter* Serina *and* Chamont.]

SERINA.
    My father!
ACASTO.   My heart's darling!
SERINA.   Let my knees
    Fix to the earth. Ne'er let my eyes have rest,
    But wake and weep till Heaven restore my father.
ACASTO.
    Rise to my arms, and thy kind prayers are answered,   100
    For thou'rt a wondrous extract of all goodness;
    Born for my joy, and no pain's felt when near thee.
    Chamont!

---

78. *spleen*] ill-nature, spite, malice.
94. *laugh ye out on't*] mock you so as to undermine religious faith.

CHAMONT.

My lord, may't prove not an unlucky omen!
Many I see are waiting round about you;   105
And I am come to ask a blessing too.

ACASTO.

Mayst thou be happy!

CHAMONT.   Where?

ACASTO.   In all thy wishes.

CHAMONT.

Confirm me so, and make this fair one mine.
I am unpracticed in the trade of courtship,
And know not how to deal love out with art.   110
Onsets in love seem best like those in war,
Fierce, resolute, and done with all the force.
So I would open my whole heart at once,
And pour out the abundance of my soul.

ACASTO.

What says Serina? Canst thou love a soldier?   115
One born to honor and to honor bred?
One that has learned to treat ev'n foes with kindness?
To wrong no good man's fame, nor praise himself?

SERINA.

Oh, name not love, for that's allied to joy,
And joy must be a stranger to my heart   120
When you're in danger. May Chamont's good fortune
Render him lovely to some happier maid!
Whilst I at friendly distance see him blest,
Praise the kind gods, and wonder at his virtues.

ACASTO.

Chamont, pursue her, conquer, and possess her,   125
And as my son, a third of all my fortune
Shall be thy lot.
But keep thy eyes from wand'ring, man of frailty!
Beware the dangerous beauty of the wanton;
Shun their enticements; ruin, like a vulture,   130
Waits on their conquests. Falsehood too's their business;
They put false beauty off to all the world;
Use false endearments to the fools that love 'em,
And when they marry, to their silly husbands

---

134. *silly*] innocent, unsuspecting.

They bring false virtue, broken fame, and fortune.   135

MONIMIA [*aside to* Polydore].
    Hear ye that, my lord?

POLYDORE [*aside to* Monimia].
    Yes, my fair monitor. Old men always talk thus.

ACASTO.
    Chamont, you told me of some doubts that pressed you.
    Are you yet satisfied that I am your friend?

CHAMONT.
    My lord, I would not lose that satisfaction   140
    For any blessing I could wish for.
    As to my fears, already I have lost 'em;
    They ne'er shall vex me more, nor trouble you.

ACASTO.
    I thank you. [*To* Monimia.] Daughter, you must do so
        too.—
    My friends, 'tis late, or we would yet be company,   145
    For my disorder seems all past and over,
    And I methinks begin to feel new health.

CASTALIO.
    Would you but rest, it might restore you quite.

ACASTO.
    Yes, I'll to bed. Old men must humor weakness.
    Let me have music then, to lull and chase   150
    This melancholy thought of death away.
    Good night, my friends, Heaven guard ye all! Good
        night.
    Tomorrow early, we'll salute the day,
    Find out new pleasures, and redeem lost time.
                    Exeunt all but Chamont *and* Chaplain.

CHAMONT.
    Hist! hist! Sir Gravity! A word with you.   155

CHAPLAIN.
    With me, sir?

CHAMONT.
    If you're at leisure, sir, we'll waste an hour.
    'Tis yet too soon to sleep, and 'twill be charity
    To lend your conversation to a stranger.

CHAPLAIN.

Sir, you are a soldier?   160

CHAMONT.

Yes.

CHAPLAIN.

I love a soldier, and had been one myself, but my old parents would make me what you see of me. Yet I'm honest, for all I wear black.

CHAMONT [*aside*].

And that's a wonder.—Have you had long dependence 165 on this family?

CHAPLAIN.

I have not thought it so, because my time's spent pleasantly. My lord's not haughty nor imperious, nor I gravely whimsical. He has good nature, and I have manners. His sons too are civil to me, because I do not pre- 170 tend to be wiser than they are; I meddle with no man's business but my own; I rise in a morning early, study moderately, eat and drink cheerfully, live soberly, take my innocent pleasures freely; so meet with respect, and am not the jest of the family.   175

CHAMONT.

I'm glad you are so happy.

[*Aside.*] A pleasant fellow this, and may be useful.—

Knew you my father, the old Chamont?

CHAPLAIN.

I did, and was most sorry when we lost him.

CHAMONT.

Why? Didst thou love him?   180

CHAPLAIN.

Ev'rybody loved him; besides he was my master's friend.

CHAMONT.

I could embrace thee for that very notion.

If thou didst love my father, I could think

Thou wouldst not be an enemy to me.

---

162. old] *Q1; om. Q2.*   174. so] *Q2–3;* so I *Q1.*
163. I'm] *Q1;* I am *Q2.*   181. besides] *Q1;* beside *Q2.*

160. *soldier*] Chamont wears the regulation scarlet of an English regiment, in contrast to the Chaplain's black.

CHAPLAIN.
    I can be no man's foe.
CHAMONT.   Then prithee tell me,   185
    Think'st thou the Lord Castalio loves my sister?
    Nay never start. Come, come, I know thy office
    Opens thee all the secrets of the family.
    Then, if thou art honest, use this freedom kindly.
CHAPLAIN.
    Love your sister?   190
CHAMONT.
    Ay, love her.
CHAPLAIN.
    Sir, I never asked him,
    And wonder you should ask it me.
CHAMONT.
    Nay, but th'art an hypocrite. Is there not one
    Of all thy tribe that's honest in your schools?   195
    The pride of your superiors makes ye slaves.
    Ye all live loathsome, sneaking, servile lives,
    Not free enough to practice generous truth,
    Though ye pretend to teach it to the world.

CHAPLAIN.
    I would deserve a better thought from you.   200
CHAMONT.
    If thou wouldst have me not contemn thy office
    And character, think all thy brethren knaves,
    Thy trade a cheat, and thou its worst professor—
    Inform me; for I tell thee, priest, I'll know.

CHAPLAIN.
    Either he loves her, or he much has wronged her.   205

CHAMONT.
    How wronged her? Have a care, for this may lay
    A scene of mischief to undo us all.
    But tell me, wronged her saidst thou?
CHAPLAIN.   Ay, sir, wronged her.
CHAMONT.
    This is a secret worth a monarch's fortune.
    What shall I give thee for't, thou dear physician   210
    Of sickly souls? Unfold this riddle to me,
    And comfort mine—

CHAPLAIN.
   I would hide nothing from you willingly.

CHAMONT.
   Nay, then again thou'rt honest. Wouldst thou tell me?

CHAPLAIN.
   Yes, if I durst—

CHAMONT.   Why, what affrights thee?

CHAPLAIN.   You do,   215
   Who are not to be trusted with the secret.

CHAMONT.
   Why, I am no fool.

CHAPLAIN.   So indeed you say.

CHAMONT.
   Prithee, be serious then.

CHAPLAIN.   You see I am so;
   And hardly shall be mad enough tonight
   To trust you with my ruin.

CHAMONT.   Art thou then   220
   So far concerned in't? What has been thy office?
   Curse on that formal steady villain's face!
   Just so do all bawds look. Nay, bawds, they say,
   Can pray upon occasion, talk of Heav'n,
   Turn up their goggling eyeballs, rail at vice,   225
   Dissemble, lie, and preach like any priest.
   Art thou a bawd?

CHAPLAIN.   Sir, I'm not often used thus.

CHAMONT.
   Be just then.

CHAPLAIN.   So I will be to the trust
   That's laid upon me.

CHAMONT.   By the rev'renced soul
   Of that great honest man that gave me being,   230
   Tell me but what thou know'st concerns my honor,
   And if I e'er reveal it to thy wrong,
   May this good sword ne'er do me right in battle!
   May I ne'er know that blessed peace of mind,
   That dwells in good and pious men like thee!   235

228. will] *Q1; om. Q2–3.*

CHAPLAIN.
    I see your temper's moved, and I will trust you.
CHAMONT.
    Wilt thou?
CHAPLAIN.   I will; but if it ever 'scape you—
CHAMONT.
    It never shall.
CHAPLAIN.   Swear then.
CHAMONT.   I do. By all
    That's dear to me, by th'honor of my name,
    And that Power I serve, it never shall.   240
CHAPLAIN.
    Then this good day, when all the house was busy,
    When mirth and kind rejoicing filled each room,
    As I was walking in the grove I met them—
CHAMONT.
    What, met them in the grove together? Tell me,
    How? Walking, standing, sitting, lying? Hah!   245
CHAPLAIN.
    I by their own appointment met them there,
    Received their marriage vows and joined their hands.
CHAMONT.
    How! Married?
CHAPLAIN.   Yes, sir.
CHAMONT.   Then my soul's at peace.
    But why would you delay so long to give it?
CHAPLAIN.
    Not knowing what reception it may find   250
    With old Acasto, may be I was too cautious
    To trust the secret from me.
CHAMONT [aside.]   What's the cause
    I cannot guess; though 'tis my sister's honor,
    I do not like this marriage,
    Huddled i'th' dark and done at too much venture.   255
    The business looks with an unlucky face.
    [To the Chaplain.] Keep still the secret, for it ne'er shall
        'scape me,
    Not ev'n to them, the new-matched pair. Farewell.
    Believe my truth and know me for thy friend.   Exeunt.

47

Enter Castalio *and* Monimia.

CASTALIO.

    Young Chamont, and the Chaplain? Sure 'tis they!   260
    No matter what's contrived, or who consulted,
    Since my Monimia's mine; though this sad look
    Seems no good boding omen to our bliss;
    Else, prithee, tell me why that look cast down?
    Why that sad sigh, as if thy heart were breaking?   265

MONIMIA.

    Castalio, I am thinking what we've done.
    The Heavenly Powers were sure displeased today,
    For at the ceremony, as we stood,
    And as your hand was kindly joined with mine,
    As the good priest pronounced the sacred words,   270
    Passion grew big and I could not forbear;
    Tears drowned my eyes, and trembling seized my soul.
    What should that mean?

CASTALIO.   Oh, thou art tender all!

    Gentle and kind as sympathizing Nature!
    When a sad story has been told, I've seen   275
    Thy little breasts, with soft compassion swelled,
    Shove up and down and heave like dying birds;
    But now let fear be banished; think no more
    Of danger, for there's safety in my arms;
    Let them receive thee. Heav'n, grow jealous now!   280
    Sure she's too good for any mortal creature!
    I could grow wild, and praise thee ev'n to madness.
    But wherefore do I dally with my bliss?
    The night's far spent and day draws on apace;
    To bed, my love, and wake till I come thither.   285

        [*Enter*] Polydore *at the door.*

POLYDORE [*aside*].

    So hot, my brother?

MONIMIA.   'Twill be impossible.

    You know your father's chamber's next to mine,
    And the least noise will certainly alarm him.

286.1. *the door*] one of the two permanent doors set behind the proscenium doors which opened onto the stage in front of the curtain. See
Appendix B.

CASTALIO.

   Impossible? Impossible? alas!
   Is't possible to live one hour without thee?   290
   Let me behold those eyes, they'll tell me truth.
   Hast thou no longing? Art thou still the same
   Cold icy virgin? No; th'art altered quite.
   Haste, haste to bed, and let loose all thy wishes.

MONIMIA.

   'Tis but one night, my lord, I pray be ruled.   295

CASTALIO.

   Try if th'ast power to stop a flowing tide,
   Or in a tempest make the seas be calm,
   And when that's done, I'll conquer my desires.
   No more, my blessing. What shall be the sign?
   When shall I come? For to my joys I'll steal   300
   As if I ne'er had paid my freedom for them.

MONIMIA.

   Just three soft strokes upon the chamber door,
   And at that signal you shall gain admittance;
   But speak not the least word, for if you should,
   'Tis surely heard, and all will be betrayed.   305

CASTALIO.

   Oh, doubt it not, Monimia. Our joys
   Shall be as silent as the ecstatic bliss
   Of souls that by intelligence converse.
   Immortal pleasures shall our senses drown;
   Thought shall be lost, and ever pow'r dissolved.   310
   Away, my love! First take this kiss. Now haste.
   I long for that to come, yet grudge each minute past.

                            Exit Monimia.

   My brother wand'ring too so late this way?

POLYDORE.

   Castalio!

CASTALIO.   My Polydore, how dost thou?
   How does our father? Is he well recovered?   315

308–10. *intelligence . . . Thought*] approximately the distinction drawn in
scholastic philosophy between "intuition," the immediate knowledge ascribed to spiritual beings, and "discursive reason," which passes from
premise to conclusion. Cf. Milton, *Paradise Lost*, 5, 488–91.

POLYDORE.

    I left him happily reposed to rest;
    He's still as gay as if his life were young.
    But how does fair Monimia?

CASTALIO.   Doubtless well.

    A cruel beauty with her conquests pleased
    Is always joyful and her mind in health.   320

POLYDORE.

    Is she the same Monimia still she was?
    May we not hope she's made of mortal mould?

CASTALIO.

    She's not a woman else—
    Though I'm grown weary of this tedious hoping;
    W'ave in a barren desert strayed too long.   325

POLYDORE.

    Yet may relief be unexpected found,
    And love's sweet manna cover all the field.
    Met ye today?

CASTALIO.   No, she has still avoided me.

    Her brother too is jealous of her grown,
    And has been hinting something to my father.   330
    I wish I'd never meddled with the matter,
    And would enjoin thee, Polydore—

POLYDORE.   To what?

CASTALIO.

    To leave this peevish beauty to herself.

POLYDORE.

    What, quit my love? As soon I'd quit my post
    In fight, and like a coward run away.   335
    No, by my stars, I'll chase her till she yields
    To me, or meets her rescue in another.

CASTALIO.

    Nay, she has beauty that might shake the leagues
    Of mighty kings and set the world at odds;
    But I have wondrous reasons on my side   340
    That would persuade thee, were they known.

POLYDORE.   Then speak 'em.

    What are they? Came ye to her window here

---

342. *her window here*] one of the permanent stage windows built over
each of the proscenium doors.

To learn 'em now? Castalio, have a care;
Use honest dealing with your friend and brother.
Believe me, I'm not with my love so blinded,   345
But can discern your purpose to abuse me.
Quit your pretenses to her.
CASTALIO.   Grant I do.
You love capitulation, Polydore,
And but upon conditions would oblige me.
POLYDORE.
You say you've reasons. Why are they concealed?   350
CASTALIO.
Tomorrow I may tell you.
It is a matter of such circumstance,
As I must well consult e'er I reveal.
But, prithee, cease to think I would abuse thee,
Till more be known.
POLYDORE.   When you, Castalio, cease   355
To meet Monimia unknown to me,
And then deny it slavishly, I'll cease
To think Castalio faithless to his friend.
Did I not see you part this very moment?
CASTALIO.
It seems you've watched me then?
POLYDORE.   I scorn the office. 360
CASTALIO.
Prithee, avoid a thing thou mayst repent.
POLYDORE.
That is henceforward making leagues with you.
CASTALIO.
Nay, if y'are angry, Polydore, good night.
                                        Exit Castalio.
POLYDORE.
Good night, Castalio, if y'are in such haste.
[*Solus.*] He little thinks I've overheard th'appoint-
    ment,   365
But to his chamber's gone to wait a while,
Then come and take possession of my love.
This is the utmost point of all my hope:
Or now she must, or never can be mine.
Oh, for a means now how to counterplot   370

51

And disappoint this happy elder brother!
In everything we do, or undertake,
He soars above me, mount what height I can,
And keeps the start he got of me in birth.
Cordelio!

Enter Page.

PAGE.   My lord?

POLYDORE.   Come hither, boy.   375
Thou hast a pretty forward lying face,
And mayst in time expect preferment. Canst thou
Pretend to secrecy? Cajole and flatter
Thy master's follies and assist his pleasures?

PAGE.

My lord, I could do anything for you,   380
And ever be a very faithful boy.
Command whate'er's your pleasure, I'll observe:
Be it to run, or watch, or to convey
A letter to a beauteous lady's bosom;
At least I am not dull, and soon should learn.   385

POLYDORE.

'Tis pity then thou shouldst not be employed.
Go to my brother. He's in's chamber now,
Undressing and preparing for his rest.
Find out some means to keep him up a while;
Tell him a pretty story that may please   390
His ear. Invent a tale, no matter what.
If he should ask of me, tell him I'm gone
To bed, and sent you there to know his pleasure,
Whether he'll hunt to-morrow. [*Aside.*] Well said, Poly-
     dore;
Dissemble with thy brother! [*To* Page.]   That's one
     point.   395
But do not leave him till he's in his bed;
Or if he chance to walk again this way,
Follow, and do not quit him, but seem fond
To do him little offices of service.
Perhaps at last it may offend him; then   400

383. or watch] *Q1;* or to watch *Q2.*

Retire and wait till I come in. Away!
Succeed in this, and be employed again.

PAGE.

Doubt not, my lord. He has been always kind
To me; would often set me on his knees,
Then give me sweetmeats, call me pretty boy,   405
And ask me what the maids talked of at nights.

POLYDORE.

Run quickly then, and prosperous be thy wishes.

Exit Page.

Here I'm alone and fit for mischief. Now
To cheat this brother. Will't be honest that
I heard the sign she ordered him to give?   410
Oh, for the art of Proteus but to change
The happy Polydore to blest Castalio!
She's not so well acquainted with him yet,
But I may fit her arms as well as he.
Then, when I'm happily possessed of more   415
Than sense can think, all loosened into joy,
To hear my disappointed brother come
And give the unregarded signal. Oh!
What a malicious pleasure will that be!
"Just three soft strokes against the chamber door;   420
But speak not the least word, for if you should,
It is surely heard, and we are both betrayed."
How I adore a mistress that contrives
With care to lay the business of her joys!
One that has wit to charm the very soul,   425
And gives a double relish to delight.
Blest Heav'n, assist me but in this dear hour,
And my kind stars be but propitious now;
Dispose of me hereafter as you please.
Monimia! Monimia!

Gives the sign.

FLORELLA (*at the window*). Who's there?   430

POLYDORE.

    'Tis I.

430–37. S.P. (and S.D.) FLORELLA]
Q1–4; MAID. *W1.*

FLORELLA. My Lord Castalio?

POLYDORE.   The same.

　　How does my love, my dear Monimia?

FLORELLA.   Oh!

　　She wonders much at your unkind delay!
　　You've stayed so long that at each little noise
　　The wind but makes, she asks if you are coming.   435

POLYDORE.

　　Tell her I'm here, and let the door be opened.

　　　　　　　　　　Florella *descends*.

　　Now boast, Castalio, triumph now and tell
　　Thyself strange stories of a promised bliss.

　　　　　　　　　　The door unbolts.

　　It opens, hah! What means my trembling flesh!
　　Limbs, do your office and support me well.   440
　　Bear me to her, then fail me if you can.   [*Exit.*]

　　　　　　　　Enter Castalio *and* Page.

PAGE.

　　Indeed, my lord, 'twill be a lovely morning!
　　Pray let us hunt.

CASTALIO.   Go, you're an idle prattler.

　　I'll stay at home tomorrow. If your lord
　　Thinks fit, he may command my hounds. Go, leave me,   445
　　I must to bed.

PAGE.   I'll wait upon your lordship,

　　If you think fit, and sing you to repose.

CASTALIO.

　　No, my kind boy; the night is too far wasted;
　　My senses too are quite disrobed of thought,
　　And ready all with me to go to rest.   450
　　Good night: commend me to my brother.

PAGE.   Oh!

　　You never heard the last new song I learned.
　　It is the finest, prettiest song indeed,
　　Of my lord and my lady, you know who, that were
　　caught together, you know where, my lord, indeed it is. 455

CASTALIO.

　　You must be whipped, youngster, if you get such songs

as those are. [*Aside.*] What means this boy's impertinence
tonight?

PAGE.

Why, what must I sing, pray, my dear lord?

CASTALIO.

Psalms, child, psalms.   460

PAGE.

Oh, dear me! Boys that go to school learn psalms, but
pages that are better bred sing lampoons.

CASTALIO.

Well, leave me; I'm weary.

PAGE.

Oh, but you promised me last time I told you what color
my Lady Monimia's stockings were of and that she gar-   465
tered them above the knee, that you would give me a
little horse to go hunting upon, so you did. I'll tell you no
more stories, except you keep your word with me.

CASTALIO.

Well, go, you trifler, and tomorrow ask me.

PAGE.

Indeed, my lord, I can't abide to leave you.   470

CASTALIO.

Why, wert thou instructed to attend me?

PAGE.

No, no, indeed, indeed, my lord, I was not—but I know
what I know—

CASTALIO.

What dost thou know? [*Aside.*] Death! What can all this
mean?   475

PAGE.

Oh, I know who loves somebody.

CASTALIO.

What's that to me, boy?

PAGE.

Nay, I know who loves you too.

CASTALIO.

That is a wonder; prithee, tell it me.

PAGE.

'Tis—'tis—I know who—but will you give me the horse   480
then?

CASTALIO.

    I will, my child.

PAGE.

    It is my Lady Monimia, look you—but don't you tell her
    I told you; she'll give me no more playthings then. I
    heard her say so as she lay a-bed, man.   485

CASTALIO.

    Talked she of me when in her bed, Cordelio?

PAGE.

    Yes, and I sung her the song you made too. And she did
    so sigh, and so look with her eyes; and her breasts did so
    lift up and down. I could have found in my heart to have
    beat 'em, for they made me ashamed.   490

CASTALIO.

    Hark! What's that noise?
    Take this, be gone, and leave me.
    You knave, you little flatterer, get you gone.

                                           Exit Page.

    Surely it was a noise. Hist! Only fancy.
    For all is hushed as Nature were retired,   495
    And the perpetual motion standing still,
    So much she from her work appears to cease,
    And every warring element's at peace;
    All the wild herds are in their coverts couched;
    The fishes to their banks or ooze repaired,   500
    And to the murmurs of the waters sleep;
    The feeling air's at rest and feels no noise,
    Except of some soft breaths among the trees,
    Rocking the harmless birds that rest upon 'em.
    'Tis now that guided by my love I go   505
    To take possession of Monimia's arms.
    Sure Polydore's by this time gone to bed.
    At midnight thus the us'rer steals untracked
    To make a visit to his hoarded gold
    And feast his eyes upon the shining mammon.   510

                      Knocks.

    She hears me not; sure she already sleeps.
    Her wishes could not brook my so long delay
    And her poor heart has beat itself to rest.

Knocks again.

Monimia! My angel—hah—not yet—
How long's the softest moment of delay   515
To a heart impatient of its pangs like mine,
In sight of ease and panting to the goal.

Knocks again.

Once more—
FLORELLA [*at the window*].
Who's there,
That comes thus rudely to disturb our rest?   520
CASTALIO.
'Tis I.
FLORELLA. Who are you, what's your name?
CASTALIO.   Suppose
The Lord Castalio.
FLORELLA.   I know you not;
The Lord Castalio has no business here.
CASTALIO.
Hah! Have a care! What can this mean?
Whoe'er thou art, I charge thee to Monimia fly;   525
Tell her I'm here and wait upon my doom.
FLORELLA.
Whoe'er you are, you may repent this outrage.
My lady must not be disturbed. Good night.
CASTALIO.
She must. Tell her she shall. Go, I'm in haste,
And bring her tidings from the state of love;   530
Th'are all in consultation met together,
How to reward my truth, and crown her vows.
FLORELLA.
Sure the man's mad—
CASTALIO.   Or this will make me so.
Obey me, or by all the wrongs I suffer,
I'll scale the window and come in by force,   535
Let the sad consequence be what it will.
                    [Florella *disappears from the window.*]
This creature's trifling folly makes me mad.

───────────────────────────

519–43. S.P. (and S.D.) FLORELLA]   527. Whoe'er you] *Q1;* who are ye
Q1–4; MAID *W1.*   *Q2.*

───────────────────────────

FLORELLA [*reappears at the window*].

    My lady's answer is, you may depart.
    She says she knows you: you are Polydore,
    Sent by Castalio as you were today,   540
    T'affront and do her violence again.

CASTALIO.

    I'll not believ't.

FLORELLA.   You may, sir.

CASTALIO.   Curses blast thee!

FLORELLA.

    Well, 'tis a fine cool evening, and I hope
    May cure the raging fever in your blood.
    Good night!

CASTALIO.   And farewell all that's just in woman!   545
    This is contrived, a studied trick to abuse
    My easy nature and torment my mind.
    Sure, now sh'has bound me fast, and means to lord it,
    To rein me hard, and ride me at her will,
    Till by degrees she shape me into fool   550
    For all her future uses. Death and torment!
    'Tis impudence to think my soul will bear it.
    Oh, I could grow ev'n wild, and tear my hair.
    'Tis well, Monimia, that thy empire's short;
    Let but tomorrow, but tomorrow come,   555
    And try if all thy arts appease my wrong;
    Till when, be this detested place my bed,   *Lies down.*
    Where I will ruminate on woman's ills,
    Laugh at myself and curse th'inconstant sex.
    Faithless Monimia! Oh, Monimia!

Enter Ernesto.

ERNESTO.   Either   560
    My sense has been deluded, or this way
    I heard the sound of sorrow. 'Tis late night,
    And none whose mind's at peace would wander now.

CASTALIO.

    Who's there?

ERNESTO.   A friend.

CASTALIO.   If thou art so, retire,
    And leave this place, for I would be alone.   565

ERNESTO.
> Castalio! My lord, why in this posture,
> Stretched on the ground? Your honest true old servant,
> Your poor Ernesto, cannot see you thus.
> Rise, I beseech you.

CASTALIO.   If thou art Ernesto,
> As by thy honesty thou seemest to be,   570
> Once leave me to my folly.

ERNESTO.   I can't leave you,
> And not the reason know of your disorders.
> Remember how, when young, I in my arms
> Have often borne you, pleased in your pleasures,
> And sought an early share in your affection?   575
> Do not discard me now, but let me serve you.

CASTALIO.
> Thou canst not serve me.

ERNESTO.   Why?

CASTALIO.   Because my thoughts
> Are full of woman. Thou, poor wretch, art past 'em.

ERNESTO.
> I hate the sex.

CASTALIO.   Then I'm thy friend, Ernesto.   *Rises.*
> I'd leave the world for him that hates a woman.   580
> Woman, the fountain of all human frailty!
> What mighty ills have not been done by woman?
> Who was't betrayed the Capitol? A woman.
> Who lost Mark Anthony the world? A woman.
> Who was the cause of a long ten years' war,   585
> And laid at last Old Troy in ashes? A woman.
> Destructive, damnable, deceitful woman.

---

583. *betrayed the Capitol*] Tarpeia, daughter of Tarpeius, governor of the citadel of Rome, opened the gates of the city to the Sabines in return for "what they carried on their left arms," meaning their gold bracelets and not the shields which they threw on her, crushing her under the weight.

584. *lost Mark Anthony the world*] Cleopatra, who fled the battle of Actium in 33 B.C.

586. *Old Troy*] Priam's Troy, as distinguished from "New Troy" or Troynovant, the name given by the early chroniclers to London, and used frequently by the writers of the Lord Mayors' Shows. Cf. Spenser, *Faerie Queene*, 3, 9. The *woman* is Helen.

Woman, to man first as a blessing giv'n
When innocence and love were in their prime!
    Happy a while in Paradise they lay;   590
    But quickly woman longed to go astray;
    Some foolish new adventure needs must prove,
    And the first devil she saw she changed her love;
    To his temptations lewdly she inclined
    Her soul, and for an apple damned mankind.   595

[Exeunt.]

ACT IV

Acasto *solus.*

ACASTO.

  Blest be the morning that has brought me health.
  A happy rest has softened pain away,
  And I'll forget it, though my mind's not well.
  A heavy melancholy clogs my heart;
  I droop and sigh I know not why. Dark dreams,   5
  Sick fancy's children, have been overbusy
  And all the night played farces in my brains.
  Methought I heard the midnight raven cry;
  Waked with th'imagined noise, my curtains seemed
  To start, and at my feet my sons appeared   10
  Like ghosts, all pale and stiff. I strove to speak,
  But could not. Suddenly the forms were lost,
  And seemed to vanish in a bloody cloud.
  'Twas odd, and for the present shook my thoughts;
  But was th'effect of my distempered blood;   15
  And when the health's disturbed, the mind's unruly.

Enter Polydore.

  Good morning, Polydore.
POLYDORE.   Heaven keep your lordship.
ACASTO.
  Have you seen Castalio today?
POLYDORE.
  My lord, 'tis early day; he's hardly risen.
ACASTO.
  Go, call him up, and meet me in the chapel.   20
                         Exit Polydore.
  I cannot think all has gone well tonight;
  For as I waking lay, and sure my sense
  Was then my own, methought I heard my son
  Castalio's voice, but it seemed low and mournful;
  Under my window too I thought I heard it.   25
  M'untoward fancy could not be deceived

2. softened] softned *Q1–4*.

0.1.] "Act IV. Scene, a saloon" (Bell).

In everything; and I will search the truth out.

Enter Monimia, *and her* Maid [, Florella].

Already up, Monimia! You rose
Thus early surely to outshine the day!
Or was there anything that crossed your rest?   30
Those were naughty thoughts that would not let you
    sleep.

MONIMIA.

Whatever are my thoughts, my lord, I've learned
By your example to correct their ills,
And morn and evening give up th'account.

ACASTO.

Your pardon, sweet one, I upbraid you not;   35
Or if I would, you are so good I could not.
Though I'm deceived, or you are more fair today,
For beauty's heightened in your cheeks, and all
Your charms seem up, and ready in your eyes.

MONIMIA.

The little share I have's so very mean   40
That it may easily admit addition.
Though you, my lord, should most of all beware
To give it too much praise, and make me proud.

ACASTO.

Proud of an old man's praises! No, Monimia!
But if my pray'rs can work thee any good,   45
Thou shalt not want the largest share of 'em.
Heard you no noise tonight?

MONIMIA.

Noise, my good lord?

ACASTO.   Ay, about midnight.

MONIMIA.

Indeed, my lord, I don't remember any.

ACASTO.

You must, sure! Went you early to rest?   50

MONIMIA.

About the wonted hour. [*Aside.*] Why this inquiry?

45. pray'rs can work thee] *Q1;*
pray'rs can do you *Q2–3.*

ACASTO.
And went your maid to bed too?
MONIMIA.   My lord, I guess so;
I've seldom known her disobey my orders.
ACASTO.
Sure goblins then, fairies haunt the dwelling.
I'll have inquiry made through all the house,   55
But I'll find out the cause of these disorders.
Good day to thee, Monimia; I'll to chapel.

MONIMIA.
I'll but dispatch some orders to my woman,
And wait upon your lordship there.   *Exit* Acasto.
[*To* Florella.] I fear the priest has played us false; if so   60
My poor Castalio loses all for me.
I wonder though, he made such haste to leave me.
Was't not unkind, Florella? Surely 'twas!
He scarce afforded one kind parting word,
But went away so cold. The kiss he gave me   65
Seemed the forced complement of sated love.
Would I had never married!
FLORELLA.   Why?
MONIMIA.   Methinks
The scene's quite altered. I am not the same;
I've bound up for myself a weight of cares,
And how the burden will be borne, none knows.   70
A husband may be jealous, rigid, false;
And should Castalio e'er prove so to me,
So tender is my heart, so nice my love,
'Twould ruin and distract my rest forever.
FLORELLA.
Madam, he's coming.
MONIMIA.   Where, Florella? Where?   75
Is he returning? To my chamber lead.
I'll meet him there. The mysteries of our love
Should be kept private, as religious rites,

54. goblins] *Q1;* goblings *Q2–3.*   67–75. S.P. FLORELLA] *Q1–4;* MAID
59. S.D.] *on l. 57 in Q1–4.*   *W1.*

From the unhallowed view of common eyes.

Exeunt Monimia *and* Florella.

Enter Castalio.

CASTALIO.

Wished morning's come! And now upon the plains 80
And distant mountains, where they feed their flocks,
The happy shepherds leave their homely huts,
And with their pipes proclaim the new-born day.
The lusty swain comes with his well-filled scrip
Of healthful viands, which, when hunger calls, 85
With much content and appetite he eats,
To follow in the fields his daily toil,
And dress the grateful glebe that yields him fruits.
The beasts that under the warm hedges slept,
And weathered out the cold bleak night, are up, 90
And looking towards the neighb'ring pastures, raise
The voice, and bid their fellow brutes good morrow.
The cheerful birds, too, on the tops of trees,
Assemble all in choirs, and with their notes
Salute and welcome up the rising sun. 95
There's no condition sure so cursed as mine.
I'm married. 'Sdeath! I'm sped. How like a dog
Looked Hercules, thus to a distaff chained!
Monimia! Oh, Monimia!

Enter Monimia, *and* Maid [Florella].

MONIMIA.   I come,
I fly to my adored Castalio's arms, 100
My wishes' lord. May ever morn begin
Like this, and with our days our loves renew.

---

101. ever] *Q2;* every *Q1.*

79.2.] To avoid the appearance of a false entry for Monimia at l. 99,
acting versions insert "Scene, a Chamber. Enter Castalio" (Bell).
88. *glebe*] a piece of cultivated land producing crops.
98. *Hercules . . . distaff*] Hercules was sold as a slave to Omphale, Queen
of Lydia. He became so enamored of her that he dressed in the flowing
garments of a woman and sat among the maids spinning wool, while she
wore his lion-skin, armed herself with his club, and on occasion struck him
with it for his awkwardness in holding the distaff.

Now I may hope y'are satisfied—
Looking languishingly on him.
CASTALIO.   I am
Well satisfied, that thou are— oh—
MONIMIA.   What? Speak—
Art thou not well, Castalio? Come, lean   105
Upon my breasts and tell me where's thy pain.
CASTALIO.
'Tis here! 'Tis in my head; 'tis in my heart,
'Tis everywhere; it rages like a madness,
And I most wonder how my reason holds.
Nay, wonder not, Monimia; the slave   110
You thought you had secured within my breast
Is grown a rebel, and has broke his chain;
And now he walks there like a lord at large.
MONIMIA.
Am I not then your wife, your loved Monimia?
I once was so, or I've most strangely dreamt.   115
What ails my love?
CASTALIO.   Whate'er thy dreams have been,
Thy waking thoughts ne'er meant Castalio well.
No more, Monimia, of your sex's arts;
They are useless all. I'm not that pliant tool,
That necessary utensil you'd make me.   120
I know my charter better. I am man,
Obstinate man; and will not be enslaved.
MONIMIA.
You shall not fear't. Indeed, my nature's easy;
I'll ever live your most obedient wife,
Nor ever any privilege pretend   125
Beyond your will, for that shall be my law.
Indeed I will not.
CASTALIO.   Nay, you shall not, madam.
By yon bright Heav'n, you shall not. All the day
I'll play the tyrant, and at night forsake thee,
Till by afflictions and continued cares,   130
I've worn thee to a homely household drudge.
Nay, if I've any too, thou shalt be made
Subservient to all my looser pleasures,
For thou hast wronged Castalio.

MONIMIA.   No more!
  Oh, kill me here, or tell me my offense;   135
  I'll never quit you else, but on these knees,   [*Kneels.*]
  Thus follow you all day, till th'are worn bare,
  And hang upon you like a drowning creature.
  Castalio—
CASTALIO.   Away! Last night, last night—
MONIMIA.
  It was our wedding night.
CASTALIO.   No more! Forget it—   140
MONIMIA.
  Why? Do you then repent?
CASTALIO.   I do.
MONIMIA.   Oh Heaven!
  And will you leave me thus? Help, help, Florella—

   He drags her to the door and breaks from her. [*Exit* Castalio.]

  Help me to hold this yet loved cruel man.
  Oh, my heart breaks—I'm dying—oh—stand off—
              [Florella *tries to assist her to rise.*]
  I'll not indulge this woman's weakness; still   145
  Chafed, and fomented, let my heart swell on
  Till with its injuries it burst, and shake
  With the dire blow this prison to the earth.
FLORELLA.
  What sad mistake has been the cause of this?
MONIMIA.
  Castalio! Oh, how often has he swore   150
  Nature should change, the sun and stars grow dark,
  E'er he would falsify his vows to me.
  Make haste, confusion, then; sun, lose they light,
  And stars drop dead with sorrow to the earth,
  For my Castalio's false—
FLORELLA.   Unhappy day!   155
MONIMIA.
  False as the wind, the water, or the weather;
  Cruel as tigers o'er their trembling prey.
  I feel him in my breast, he tears my heart,

150–55. S.P. FLORELLA] *Q1–4;*
MAID *W1.*

And at each sigh he drinks the gushing blood.
Must I be long in pain?   160

[*Sits down. Exit* Florella.]

Enter Chamont.

CHAMONT.
In tears, Monimia!
MONIMIA.   Whoe'er thou art,
Leave me alone to my beloved despair.
CHAMONT.
Lift up thy eyes, and see who comes to cheer thee.
Tell me the story of thy wrongs, and then
See if my soul has rest till thou hast justice.   165
MONIMIA.
My brother!
CHAMONT.   Yes, Monimia, if thou think'st
That I deserve the name, I am thy brother.
MONIMIA.
Oh, Castalio!
CHAMONT.
Hah!
Name me that name again! My soul's on fire   170
Till I know all. There's meaning in that name.
I know he is thy husband. Therefore trust me
With all the following truth—
MONIMIA.   Indeed, Chamont,
There's nothing in it but the fault of nature.
I'm often thus seized suddenly with grief;   175
I know not why.
CHAMONT.   You use me ill, Monimia;
And I might think with justice most severely
Of this unfaithful dealing with your brother.
MONIMIA.
Truly, I am not to blame. Suppose I'm fond
And grieve for what as much may please another?   180
Should I upbraid the dearest friend on earth
For the first fault? You would not do so, would you?
CHAMONT.
Not if I'd cause to think it was a friend.

167. thy] *Q2; om. Q1.*

MONIMIA.

    Why do you then call this unfaithful dealing?
    I ne'er concealed my soul from you before.   185
    Bear with me now, and search my wounds no farther,
    For every probing pains me to the heart.

CHAMONT.

    'Tis sign there's danger in't, and must be prevented.
    Where's your new husband? Still that thought disturbs
       you!
    What, only answer me with tears? Castalio!   190
    Nay, now they stream.
    Cruel, unkind Castalio! Is't not so?

MONIMIA.

    I cannot speak. Grief flows so fast upon me,
    It chokes, and will not let me tell the cause.
    Oh!   195

CHAMONT.

    My Monimia! To my soul thou'rt dear,
    As honor to my name; dear as the light
    To eyes but just restored and healed of blindness.
    Why wilt thou not repose within my breast
    The anguish that torments thee?

MONIMIA.   Oh, I dare not.   200

CHAMONT.

    I have no friend but thee; we must confide
    In one another. Two unhappy orphans,
    Alas, we are; and when I see thee grieve,
    Methinks it is a part of me that suffers.

MONIMIA.

    Oh, shouldst thou know the cause of my lamenting,   205
    I'm satisfied, Chamont, that thou wouldst scorn me;
    Thou wouldst despise the abject lost Monimia,
    No more wouldst praise this beauty. But
    When in some cell distracted, as I shall be,
    Thou seest me lie: these unregarded locks   210
    Matted like furies' tresses; my poor limbs
    Chained to the ground; and 'stead of the delights
    Which happy lovers taste, my keeper's stripes,
    A bed of straw, and a coarse wooden dish
    Of wretched sustenance— When thus thou seest me,   215

Prithee have charity and pity for me.
Let me enjoy this thought.
CHAMONT.   Why wilt thou rack
My soul so long, Monimia? Ease me quickly,
Or thou wilt run me into madness first.
MONIMIA.
Could you be secret?
CHAMONT.   Secret as the grave.   220
MONIMIA.
But when I've told you, will you keep your fury
Within its bounds? Will you not do some rash
And horrid mischief? For, indeed, Chamont,
You would not think how hardly I've been used
From a near friend; from one that has my soul   225
A slave, and therefore treats it like a tyrant.
CHAMONT.
I will be calm. But has Castalio wronged thee?
Has he already wasted all his love?
What has he done? Quickly, for I'm all trembling
With expectation of a horrid tale.   230
MONIMIA.
Oh, could you think it!
CHAMONT.   What?
MONIMIA.   I fear he'll kill me.
CHAMONT.
Hah!
MONIMIA.
Indeed, I do; he's strangely cruel to me,
Which, if it lasts, I'm sure must break my heart.
CHAMONT.
What has he done?
MONIMIA.   Most barbarously used me;   235
Nothing so kind as he, when in my arms:
In thousand kisses, tender sighs and joys,
Not to be thought again, the night was wasted.
At dawn of day, he rose and left his conquest;
But when we met, and I with open arms   240
Ran to embrace the lord of all my wishes,

217. thou] *Q1; om. Q2.*

Oh, then—
CHAMONT.   Go on!
MONIMIA.   He threw me from his breast,
   Like a detested sin.
CHAMONT.   How!
MONIMIA.   As I hung too
   Upon his knees, and begged to know the cause,
   He dragged me like a slave upon the earth,   245
   And had no pity on my cries.
CHAMONT.   How! Did he
   Dash thee disdainfully away with scorn?
MONIMIA.
   He did; and more, I fear, will ne'er be friends,
   Though I still love him with unbated passion.
CHAMONT.
   What, throw thee from him!   250
MONIMIA.
   Yes, indeed he did.
CHAMONT.   So may this arm
   Throw him to the earth, like a dead dog despised!
   Lameness and leprosy, blindness and lunacy,
   Poverty, shame, pride, and the name of villain
   Light on me, if, Castalio, I forgive thee.   255
MONIMIA.
   Nay, now, Chamont, art thou unkind as he is.
   Didst thou not promise me thou wouldst be calm?
   Keep my disgrace concealed? Why shouldst thou kill
     him?
   By all my love, this arm should do him vengeance.
   Alas, I love him still; and though I ne'er   260
   Clasp him again within these longing arms,
   Yet bless him, bless him, gods, where'er he goes.

Enter Acasto.

ACASTO.
   Sure some ill fate is towards me. In my house
   I only meet with oddness and disorder.
   Each vassal has a wild distracted face,   265
   And looks as full of business as a blockhead

In times of danger. Just this moment
I met Castalio too—
CHAMONT.
Then you met a villain.
ACASTO.   270
Hah!
CHAMONT.
Yes, a villain.
ACASTO.   Have a care, young soldier,
How thou'rt too busy with Acasto's fame.
I have a sword, my arm's good old acquaintance.
Villain, to thee—
CHAMONT.   Curse on thy scandalous age
Which hinders me to rush upon thy throat   275
And tear the root up of that cursed bramble.
ACASTO.
Ungrateful ruffian! Sure my good old friend
Was ne'er thy father. Nothing of him's in thee.
What have I done in my unhappy age
To be thus used? I scorn to upbraid thee, boy,   280
But I could put thee in remembrance—
CHAMONT.   Do.
ACASTO.
I scorn it.
CHAMONT.   No, I'll calmly hear the story,
For I would fain know all, to see which scale
Weighs most— Hah! Is not that good old Acasto?
What have I done? Can you forgive this folly?   285
ACASTO.
Why dost thou ask it?
CHAMONT.   'Twas the rude o'erflowing
Of too much passion. Pray, my lord, forgive me.   *Kneels.*
ACASTO.
Mock me not, youth; I can revenge a wrong.

---

269. *villain*] Chamont, on the forestage facing the audience, does not
recognize Acasto, who enters from the back.
274. *scandalous*] Acasto's age is a "stumbling block" to vengeance by a
much younger man, and to wreak vengeance on him would therefore be
"an occasion of offence" and "bring discredit" on Chamont's class or
position (*OED*).

CHAMONT.

    I know it well. But for this thought of mine,
    Pity a madman's frenzy and forget it.   290

ACASTO.

    I will; but henceforth, prithee, be more kind.   *Raises him.*
    Whence came the cause?

CHAMONT.   Indeed, I've been to blame;

    But I'll learn better; for you've been my father.
    You've been her father too—

                      Takes Monimia *by the hand.*

ACASTO.   Forbear the prologue,

    And let me know the substance of thy tale.   295

CHAMONT.

    You took her up a little tender flower,
    Just sprouted on a bank, which the next frost
    Had nipped; and with a careful loving hand
    Transplanted her into your own fair garden,
    Where the sun always shines. There long she flourished, 300
    Grew sweet to sense, and lovely to the eye;
    Till at the last a cruel spoiler came,
    Cropped this fair rose, and rifled all its sweetness,
    Then cast it like a loathsome weed away.

ACASTO.

    You talk to me in parables, Chamont.   305
    You may have known that I'm no wordy man.
    Fine speeches are the instruments of knaves,
    Or fools, that use 'em when they want good sense.
    But honesty
    Needs no disguise nor ornament: be plain.   310

CHAMONT.

    Your son—

ACASTO.   I've two, and both I hope have honor.

CHAMONT.

    I hope so too—but—

ACASTO.   Speak.

CHAMONT.   I must inform you,

    Once more Castalio—

ACASTO.   Still Castalio!

CHAMONT.   Yes.

    Your son Castalio has wronged Monimia.

ACASTO.
   Hah! Wronged her?
CHAMONT.   Married her.
ACASTO.   I'm sorry for't.   315
CHAMONT.
   Why sorry?
   By yon blest Heaven, there's not a lord
   But might be proud to take her to his heart.
ACASTO.
   I'll not deny't.
CHAMONT.   You dare not, by the gods,
   You dare not; all your family combined   320
   In one damned falsehood to outdo Castalio
   Dare not deny't.
ACASTO.   How has Castalio wronged her?
CHAMONT.
   Ask that of him. I say, my sister's wronged;
   Monimia, my sister, born as high
   And noble as Castalio. Do her justice,   325
   Or, by the gods, I'll lay a scene of blood
   Shall make this dwelling horrible to Nature.
   I'll do't. Hark you, my lord, your son Castalio—
   Take him to your closet, and there teach him manners.
ACASTO.
   You shall have justice.
CHAMONT.   Nay; I will have justice.   330
   Who'll sleep in safety that has done me wrong?
   My lord, I'll not disturb you to repeat
   The cause of this. I beg you, to preserve
   Your house's honor, ask it of Castalio.
ACASTO.
   I will.
CHAMONT. Till then, farewell—   *Exit* Chamont.
ACASTO.   Farewell, proud boy!   335
   Monimia—
MONIMIA.   My Lord?
ACASTO.   You are my daughter.
MONIMIA.
   I am, my lord, if you'll vouchsafe to own me.

335. *boy*] a term of contempt.

ACASTO.

    When you'll complain to me, I'll prove a father.

                                          Exit Acasto.

MONIMIA.

    Now I'm undone forever. Who on earth
    Is there so wretched as Monimia?   340
    First by Castalio cruelly forsaken;
    I've lost Acasto: his parting frowns
    May well instruct me rage is in his heart.
    I shall be next abandoned to my fortune,
    Thrust out, a naked wanderer to the world   345
    And branded for the mischievous Monimia.
    What will become of me? My cruel brother
    Is framing mischiefs too, for aught I know,
    That may produce bloodshed, and horrid murder.
    I would not be the cause of one man's death   350
    To reign the empress of the earth. Nay, more:
    I'd rather lose forever my Castalio,
    My dear, unkind Castalio.

                  Enter Polydore.

POLYDORE.

    Monimia weeping?
    So morning dews on new-blown roses lodge,   355
    By the sun's amorous heat to be exhaled.
    What mean these sighs? And why thus beats thy heart?

MONIMIA.

    Let me alone to sorrow. 'Tis a cause
    None e'er shall know; but it shall with me die.

POLYDORE.

    Happy, Monimia, he to whom these sighs,   360
    These tears, and all these languishings are paid!
    I am no stranger to your dearest secret.
    I know your heart was never meant for me;
    That jewel's for an elder brother's price.

MONIMIA.

    My lord?

POLYDORE. Nay, wonder not. Last night I heard   365
    His oaths, your vows, and to my torment saw
    Your wild embraces; heard th'appointment made.

I did, Monimia, and I cursed the sound.
Wilt thou be sworn, my love? Wilt thou be ne'er
Unkind again?
MONIMIA.   Banish such fruitless hopes.   370
Have you sworn constancy to my undoing?
Will you be ne'er my friend again?
POLYDORE.
What means my love?
MONIMIA.   Away! What meant my lord
Last night?
POLYDORE.
Is that a question now to be demanded?   375
I hope Monimia was not much displeased.
MONIMIA.
Was it well done to treat me like a prostitute?
T'assault my lodging at the dead of night
And threaten me if I denied admittance?
You said you were Castalio—
POLYDORE.   By those eyes,   380
It was the same. I spent my time much better!
I tell thee, ill-natured fair one, I was posted
To more advantage on a pleasant hill
Of springing joy, and everlasting sweetness.
MONIMIA.
Hah—have a care—
POLYDORE.   Where is the danger near me?   385
MONIMIA.
I fear y'are on a rock will wreck your quiet,
And drown your soul in wretchedness forever.
A thousand horrid thoughts crowd on my memory—
Will you be kind and answer me one question?
POLYDORE.
I'd trust thee with my life on those soft breasts!   390
Breathe out the choicest secrets of my heart
Till I had nothing in it left but love.
MONIMIA.
Nay, I'll conjure you by the gods and angels,
By the honor of your name—that's most concerned—
To tell me, Polydore, and tell me truly: 395
Where did you rest last night?

POLYDORE.   Within thy arms
   I triumphed. Rest had been my foe.
MONIMIA.   'Tis done—

                                      She faints.

POLYDORE.
   She faints— No help! Who waits? A curse
   Upon my vanity that could not keep
   The secret of my happiness in silence.   400
   Confusion! We shall be surprised anon,
   And consequently all must be betrayed—
   Monimia! She breathes— Monimia—
MONIMIA.   Well—
   Let mischiefs multiply. Let every hour
   Of my loathed life yield me increase of horror!   405
   Oh, let the sun to these unhappy eyes
   Ne'er shine again, but be eclipsed forever.
   May everything I look on seem a prodigy
   To fill my soul with terrors, till I quite
   Forget I ever had humanity   410
   And grow a curser of the works of Nature.
POLYDORE.
   What means all this?
MONIMIA.   Oh, Polydore! If all
   The friendship e'er you vowed to good Castalio
   Be not a falsehood; if you ever loved
   Your brother— You've undone yourself and me.   415
POLYDORE.
   Which way? Can ruin reach the man that's rich,
   As I am, in possession of thy sweetness?
MONIMIA.
   Oh, I'm his wife.
POLYDORE.   What says Monimia? Hah—
   Speak that again—
MONIMIA.   I am Castalio's wife.
POLYDORE.
   His married wedded wife?
MONIMIA.   Yesterday's sun   420
   Saw it performed.

416. way? Can] *Q1;* way can *Q2–4.*

76

POLYDORE.   And then have I enjoyed
    My brother's wife?
MONIMIA.   As surely as we both
    Must taste of misery, that guilt is thine.
POLYDORE.
    Must we be miserable then?
MONIMIA.
    Oh!   425
POLYDORE.
    Oh, thou mayst still be happy.
MONIMIA.   Couldst thou be
    Happy with such a weight upon thy soul?
POLYDORE.
    It may be yet a secret. I'll go try
    To reconcile and bring Castalio to thee,
    Whilst from the world I take myself away,   430
    And waste my life in penance for my sin.
MONIMIA.
    Then thou wouldst more undo me; heap a load
    Of added sins upon my wretched head.
    Wouldst thou again have me betray thy brother
    And bring pollution to his arms? Cursed thought.   435
    Oh, when shall I be mad indeed!
POLYDORE.   Nay, then,
    Let us embrace, and from this very moment
    Vow an eternal misery together.
MONIMIA.
    And wilt thou be a very faithful wretch?
    Never grow fond of cheerful peace again?   440
    Wilt with me study to be unhappy,
    And find out ways how to increase affliction?
POLYDORE.
    We'll institute new arts unknown before,
    To vary plagues and make 'em look like new ones.
    First, if the fruit of our detested joy,   445
    A child, be born, it shall be murdered—
MONIMIA.   No!
    Sure, that may live.
POLYDORE.   Why?
MONIMIA.   To become a thing

> More wretched than its parents; to be branded
> With all our infamy, and curse its birth.

POLYDORE.

> That's well contrived. Then, thus let's go together,   450
> Full of our guilt, distracted where to roam,
> Like the first wretched pair expelled their paradise.
> Let's find some place where adders nest in winter,
> Loathsome and venomous; where poisons hang
> Like gums against the walls; where witches meet   455
> By night, and feed upon some pampered imp,
> Fat with the blood of babes. There we'll inhabit,
> And live up to the height of desperation.
> Desire shall languish like a withering flower,
> And no distinction of the sex be thought of;   460
>> Horrors shall fright me from those pleasing harms,
>> And I'll no more be caught with beauty's charms;
>> But when I'm dying, take me in thy arms.

Exeunt.

ACT V

Castalio *lying on the ground.*

SONG

Come, all ye youths, whose hearts e'er bled
   By cruel beauty's pride,
Bring each a garland on his head,
   Let none his sorrows hide,
But hand in hand around me move   5
   Singing the saddest tales of love;
      And see, when your complaints ye join,
      If all your wrongs can equal mine.

The happiest mortal once was I,
   My heart no sorrows knew.   10
Pity the pain with which I die,
   But ask not whence it grew.
Yet, if a tempting fair you find
   That's very lovely, very kind,
      Though bright as Heaven whose stamp she bears,   15
      Think of my fate, and shun her snares.

CASTALIO.
See where the deer trot after one another:
Male, female, father, daughter, mother, son,
Brother and sister mingled all together.
No discontent they know, but in delightful   20
Wildness and freedom, pleasant springs, fresh herbage,
Calm harbors, lusty health and innocence
Enjoy their portion. If they see a man,
How will they turn together all and gaze
Upon the monster—   25
Once in a season, too, they taste of love.
Only the beast of reason is its slave,
And in that folly drudges all the year.

   0.1.] "Act V. Scene, a garden. Castalio lying on the ground. Soft music"
(Bell).
   1–16. *Song*] set by Francis Forcer, and published in *Choice Ayres and Songs*, The Third Book, 1681.

Enter Acasto.

ACASTO [*calling*].
    Castalio! Castalio!
CASTALIO.   Who's there
    So wretched but to name Castalio?   30
ACASTO [*aside*].
    I hope my message may succeed.
CASTALIO.   My father!
    'Tis joy to see you, though where sorrow's nourished.
ACASTO.
    I'm come in beauty's cause; you'll guess the rest.
CASTALIO.
    A woman! If you love my peace of mind,
    Name not a woman to me; but to think   35
    Of woman were enough to taint my brains
    Till they foment to madness! Oh, my father—
ACASTO.
    What ails my boy?
CASTALIO.   A woman is the thing
    I would forget, and blot from my remembrance.
ACASTO.
    Forget Monimia?
CASTALIO.   She to choose. Monimia!   40
    The very sound's ungrateful to my sense.
ACASTO.
    This might seem strange, but you I've found will
    Hide your heart from me; you dare not trust your
        father.
CASTALIO.
    No more Monimia.
ACASTO.   Is she not your wife?
CASTALIO.
    So much the worse. Who loves to hear of wife?   45
    When you would give all wordly plagues a name
    Worse than they have already, call 'em wife;
    But a new-married wife's a seeming mischief,

42. will/ Hide your] *Q1–3;* will   43. trust] *Q2;* trust to *Q1*.
hide/ Your *Ghosh*.

Full of herself. Why, what a deal of horror
Has that poor wretch to come, that wedded yesterday.   50

ACASTO.

Castalio, you must go along with me
And see Monimia.

CASTALIO.   Sure my lord but mocks me!
Go see Monimia? Pray, my lord, excuse me,
And leave the conduct of this part of life
To my own choice.

ACASTO.   I say, no more dispute.   55
Complaints are made to me that you have wronged her.

CASTALIO.

Who has complained?

ACASTO.

Her brother to my face proclaimed her wronged,
And in such terms they've warmed me.

CASTALIO.

What terms? Her brother? Heaven!   60
Where learned she that?
What, does she send her hero with defiance?
He durst not sure affront you?

ACASTO.   No, not much.
But—

CASTALIO. Speak, what said he?

ACASTO.   That thou wert a villain.
Methinks I would not have thee thought a villain.   65

CASTALIO.

Shame on the ill-mannered brute:
Your age secured him; he durst not else have said so.

ACASTO.

By my sword,
I would not see thee wronged, and bear it vilely—
Though I have passed my word she shall have justice.   70

CASTALIO.

Justice! To give her justice would undo her.
Think you this solitude I now had chosen,

61. learned she] *Q1–2;* learnt he
Q3–4; W1; Ghosh.

63. *affront*] literally, to slap in the face; openly insult, so that "satisfaction" in the duel is required.

Left joys just opening to my sense, sought here
A place to curse my fate in, measured out
My grave at length, wished to have grown one piece   75
With this cold clay—and all without a cause?

Enter Chamont.

CHAMONT.
Where is the hero famous and renowned
For wronging innocence, and breaking vows?
Whose mighty spirit, and whose stubborn heart,
No woman can appease, nor man provoke?   80
ACASTO.
I guess, Chamont, you come to seek Castalio.
CHAMONT.
I come to seek the husband of Monimia.
CASTALIO.
The slave is here.
CHAMONT.   I thought e'er now to 'ave found you
Atoning for the ills you've done Chamont;
For you have wronged the dearest part of him.   85
Monimia, young lord, weeps in this heart;
And all the tears thy injuries have drawn
From her poor eyes, are drops of blood from hence.
CASTALIO.
Then you are Chamont?
CHAMONT.   Yes, and I hope no stranger
To great Castalio.
CASTALIO.   I've heard of such a man   90
That has been very busy with my honor.
I own I'm much indebted to you, sir,
And here return the villain back again
You sent me by my father.
CHAMONT.   Thus I'll thank you.

Draws.

ACASTO.
By this good sword, who first presumes to violence   95

75. wished] *Ghosh* (wisht); wish *Q1–4.*

89. *Then you are Chamont*] the insult of the cut direct.
93. *return the villain*] return the insult.

82

Makes me his foe—   *Draws and interposes.*
　　　　(*To* Castalio.)   Young man, it once was thought
I was fit guardian of my house's honor,
And you might trust your share with me—
　　　　　　　　　　　　(*To* Chamont.) For you,
Young soldier, I must tell you, you have wronged me.
I promised you to do Monimia right,   100
And thought my word a pledge I would not forfeit;
But you, I find, would fright us to performance.

CASTALIO.
Sir, in my younger years with care you taught me
That brave revenge was due to injured honor;
Oppose not then the justice of my sword,   105
Lest you should make me jealous of your love.

CHAMONT.
Into thy father's arms thou fly'st for safety,
Because thou know'st the place is sanctified
With the remembrance of an ancient friendship.

CASTALIO.
I am a villain if I will not seek thee   110
Till I may be revenged for all the wrongs
Done me by that ungrateful fair thou plead'st for.

CHAMONT.
She wrong thee! By the fury in my heart,
Thy father's honor's not above Monimia's,
Nor was thy mother's truth and virtue fairer.   115

ACASTO.
Boy, don't disturb the ashes of the dead
With thy capricious follies. The remembrance
Of the loved creature that once filled these arms—

CHAMONT.
Has not been wronged.

CASTALIO.   It shall not.

CHAMONT.   No, nor shall
Monimia, though a helpless orphan, destitute   120
Of friends and fortune, though the unhappy sister
Of poor Chamont, whose sword is all his portion,
Be oppressed by thee, thou proud imperious traitor.

---

106. *jealous*] suspicious, doubtful.

Acasto holds Castalio back.

CASTALIO.
    Hah! Let me free.
CHAMONT.   Come both.

Enter Serina.

SERINA.   Alas! alas!
    The cause of these disorders, my Chamont?   125
    Who is't has wronged thee?
CASTALIO.   Now where art thou fled
    For shelter?
CHAMONT.   Come from thine, and see what safeguard
    Shall then betray my fears.
SERINA.   Cruel Castalio,
    Sheathe up thy angry sword, and don't affright me.
    Chamont, let once Serina calm thy breast,   130
    If any of thy friends have done thee injuries,
    I'll be revenged, and love thee better for't.
CASTALIO.
    Sir, if you'd have me think you did not take
    This opportunity to show your vanity,
    Let's meet some other time, when by ourselves   135
    We fairly may dispute our wrongs together.
CHAMONT.
    Till then, I am Castalio's friend.
CASTALIO.   Serina,
    Farewell! I wish much happiness attend you.
SERINA.
    Chamont's the dearest thing I have on earth;
    Give me Chamont, and let the world forsake me.   140
CHAMONT.
    Witness the gods, how happy I am in thee!
    No beauteous blossom of the fragrant spring,
    Though the fair child of Nature newly born,
    Can be so lovely. Angry, unkind Castalio,
    Suppose I should a while lay by my passions,   145

And be a beggar in Monimia's cause,
Might I be heard?
CASTALIO.   Sir, 'twas my last request
You would; though you I find will not be satisfied:
So, in a word, Monimia is my scorn.
She basely sent you here to try my fears;   150
That was your business.
No artful prostitute, in falsehoods practiced,
To make advantage of her coxcomb's follies,
Could have done more; disquiet vex her for't.
CHAMONT.
Farewell!   [*Exeunt* Chamont *and* Serina.]
CASTALIO.   Farewell. My father, you seem troubled.   155
ACASTO.
Would I had been absent when this boistrous brave
Came to disturb thee thus. I'm grieved I hindered
Thy just resentment. But Monimia—
CASTALIO.   Damn her.
ACASTO.
Don't curse her.
CASTALIO.   Did I?
ACASTO.   Yes.
CASTALIO.   I'm sorry for it.
ACASTO.
Methinks, if as I guess, the fault's but small,   160
It might be pardoned.
CASTALIO.   No.
ACASTO.   What has she done?
CASTALIO.
That she's my wife, may Heav'n and you forgive me.
ACASTO.
Be reconciled then.
CASTALIO.   No.
ACASTO.   Go see her.
CASTALIO.   No.
ACASTO.
I'll send and bring her hither.
CASTALIO.   No.

147. Might I] *Q1;* might it *Q2.*   160. if as] *Q2;* as if *Q1.*

85

ACASTO.   For my sake,
    Castalio, and the quiet of my age.   165
CASTALIO.
    Why will you urge a thing my nature starts at?
ACASTO.
    Prithee forgive her.
CASTALIO.   Lightnings first shall blast me.
    I tell you, were she prostrate at my feet,
    Full of her sex's best dissembled sorrows,
    And all that wondrous beauty of her own,   170
    My heart might break, but it should never soften.

                    Enter Florella.

FLORELLA.
    My lord, where are you? Oh, Castalio!
ACASTO.
    Hark—
CASTALIO.
    What's that?
FLORELLA.
    Oh, show me quickly where's Castalio.   175
ACASTO.
    Why, what's the business?
FLORELLA.   Oh, the poor Monimia!
CASTALIO.
    Hah!
ACASTO.
    What's the matter?
FLORELLA.   Hurried by despair,
    She flies with fury over all the house,
    Through every room of each apartment, crying,   180
    "Where's my Castalio? Give me my Castalio!"
    Except she sees you, sure she'll grow distracted.
CASTALIO.
    Hah! Will she? Does she name Castalio?
    And with such tenderness? Conduct me quickly
    To the poor lovely mourner. Oh, my father—   185
ACASTO.
    Then wilt thou go? Blessings attend thy purpose.

CASTALIO.
I cannot hear Monimia's soul's in sadness,
And be a man. My heart will not forget her—
But do not tell the world you saw this of me.

ACASTO.
Delay not then, but haste and cheer thy love.   190

CASTALIO.
Oh, I will throw m'impatient arms about her;
In her soft bosom sigh my soul to peace,
Till through the panting breast she finds the way
To mould my heart, and make it what she will.
Monimia, oh—

Exeunt Acasto *and* Castalio. [*Manet* Florella.]

Enter Monimia.

MONIMIA [*to* Florella]. Stand off, and give me room.   195

[*Exit* Florella.]

I will not rest till I have found Castalio,
My wishes' lord, comely as rising day;
Amidst ten thousand eminently known.
Flowers spring up where'er he treads; his eyes
Fountains of brightness cheering all about him!   200
When will they shine on me? Oh stay, my soul;
I cannot die in peace till I have seen him.

Castalio *re-enters*.

CASTALIO.
Who talks of dying with a voice so sweet
That life's in love with it?

MONIMIA.   Hark! 'Tis he that answers:
So in a camp, though at the dead of night,   205
If but the trumpet's cheerful noise is heard,
All at the signal leap from downy rest,
And every heart awakes, as mine does now.
Where art thou?

CASTALIO.
Here, my love.   210

MONIMIA.
No nearer, lest I vanish.

CASTALIO.

    Have I been in a dream then all this while?
    And art thou but the shadow of Monimia?
    Why dost thou fly me thus?

MONIMIA.

    Oh, were it possible that we could drown   215
    In dark oblivion but a few past hours,
    We might be happy.

CASTALIO.

    Is't then so hard, Monimia, to forgive
    A fault, where humble love, like mine, implores thee?
    For I must love thee, though it prove my ruin.   220
    Which way shall I court thee?
    What shall I do to be enough thy slave,
    And satisfy the lovely pride that's in thee?
    I'll kneel to thee, and weep a flood before thee;
    Yet prithee, tyrant, break not quite my heart;   225
    But when my task of penitence is done,
    Heal it again, and comfort me with love.

MONIMIA.

    If I am dumb, Castalio, and want words
    To pay thee back this mighty tenderness,
    It is because I look on thee with horror   230
    And cannot see the man I so have wronged.

CASTALIO.

    Thou hast not wronged me.

MONIMIA.   Ah! Alas, thou talk'st

    Just as thy poor heart thinks. Have not I wronged thee?

CASTALIO.

    No.

MONIMIA.

    Still thou wand'rest in the dark, Castalio,   235
    But wilt e'er long stumble on horrid danger.

CASTALIO.

    What means my love?

MONIMIA.   Couldst thou but forgive me?

CASTALIO.

    What?

MONIMIA.

    For my fault last night. Alas, thou canst not.

CASTALIO.

    I can, and do.

MONIMIA [*kneeling*]. Thus crawling on the earth   240
    Would I that pardon meet, the only thing
    Can make me view the face of Heaven with hope.

CASTALIO [*raising her*].
    Then let's draw near.

MONIMIA.   Ah me!

CASTALIO.   So in the fields,
    When the destroyer has been out for prey,
    The scattered lovers of the feathered kind,   245
    Seeking when danger's past to meet again,
    Make moan, and call, by such degrees approach;
    Till joying thus they bill and spread their wings,
    Murmuring love and joy; their fears are over.

MONIMIA.
    Yet, have a care; be not too fond of peace,   250
    Lest in pursuance of the goodly quarry,
    Thou meet a disappointment that distracts thee.

CASTALIO.
    My better angel, then do thou inform me,
    What danger threatens me, and where it lies.
    Why didst thou (prithee, smile and tell me why),   255
    When I stood waiting underneath the window,
    Quaking with fierce and violent desires—
    The dropping dews fell cold upon my head;
    Darkness enclosed, and the winds whistled round me,
    Which, with my mournful sighs, made such sad music   260
    As might have moved the hardest heart— why wert thou
    Deaf to my cries and senseless of my pains?

MONIMIA.
    Did I not beg thee to forbear inquiry?
    Read'st thou not something in my face that speaks
    Wonderful change and horror from within me?   265

CASTALIO.
    Then there is something yet which I've not known.
    What dost thou mean by horror and forbearance
    Of more inquiry? Tell me, I beg thee, tell me;
    And do not betray me to a second madness.

MONIMIA.

    Must I?

CASTALIO. If laboring in the pangs of death   270

    Thou wouldst do anything to give me ease,

    Unfold this riddle e'er my thoughts grow wild

    And let in fears of ugly form upon me.

MONIMIA.

    My heart won't let me speak it; but remember,

    Monimia, poor Monimia, tells you this: 275

    We ne'er must meet again—

CASTALIO.   What means my destiny?

    For all my good or evil fate dwells in thee.

    Ne'er meet again?

MONIMIA.   No; never.

CASTALIO.   Where's the pow'r

    On earth that dares not look like thee and say so?

    Thou art my heart's inheritance; I served   280

    A long and painful, faithful slavery for thee,

    And who shall rob me of the dear-bought blessing?

MONIMIA.

    Time will clear all; but now let this content you:

    Heav'n has decreed, and therefore I've resolved

    (With torment I must tell it thee, Castalio)   285

    Ever to be a stranger to thy love;

    In some distant country waste my life,

    And from this day to see thy face no more.

CASTALIO.

    Where am I? Sure I wander midst enchantment,

    And never more shall find the way to rest.   290

    But, oh Monimia, art th'indeed resolved

    To punish me with everlasting absence?

    Why turn'st thou from me? I'm alone already.

    Methinks I stand upon a naked beach,

    Sighing to winds, and to the seas complaining,   295

    Whilst afar off the vessel sails away,

    Where all the treasure of my soul's embarked.

    Wilt thou not turn— Oh, could those eyes but speak,

    I should know all, for love is pregnant in 'em;

    They swell, they press their beams upon me still—   300

    Wilt thou not speak? If we must part forever,

Give me but one kind word to think upon,
And please myself withal, whilst my heart's breaking.

MONIMIA.

Ah, poor Castalio!   *Exit* Monimia.

CASTALIO.   Pity, by the gods;
She pities me! Then thou wilt go eternally?   305
What means all this? Why all this stir to plague
A single wretch? If but your word can shake
This world to atoms, why so much ado
With me? Think me but dead and lay me so.

Enter Polydore.

POLYDORE.

To live, and live a torment to myself—   310
What dog would bear't that knew but his condition?
We have little knowledge, and that makes us cowards,
Because it cannot tell us what's to come.

CASTALIO.

Who's there?

POLYDORE.

Why, what art thou?

CASTALIO.

My brother Polydore!

POLYDORE.

My name is Polydore.

CASTALIO.   Canst thou inform me—

POLYDORE.

Of what?

CASTALIO.

Of my Monimia.

POLYDORE.   No. Good day.

CASTALIO.   In haste?
Methinks my Polydore appears in sadness.   320

POLYDORE.

Indeed? And so to me does my Castalio.

CASTALIO.

Do I?

POLYDORE.   Thou dost.

CASTALIO.   Alas! I've wondrous reason;
I'm strangely altered, brother, since I saw thee.

91

POLYDORE.
    Why?

CASTALIO. Oh, to tell thee would but put thy heart
    To pain. Let me embrace thee but a little,   325
    And weep upon thy neck. I would repose
    Within thy friendly bosom all my follies;
    For thou wilt pardon 'em, because th'are mine.

POLYDORE.
    Be not too credulous. Consider first,
    Friends may be false. Is there no friendship false?   330

CASTALIO.
    Why dost thou ask me that? Does this appear
    Like a false friendship, when with open arms
    And streaming eyes I run upon thy breast?
    Oh 'tis in thee alone I must have comfort.

POLYDORE.
    I fear, Castalio, I have none to give thee.

CASTALIO.
    Dost thou not love me then?   Oh, more than life.

POLYDORE.
    I never had a thought of my Castalio
    Might wrong the friendship we had vowed together.
    Hast thou dealt so by me?

CASTALIO.   I hope I have.

POLYDORE.
    Then tell me, why this mourning, this disorder?   340

CASTALIO.
    Oh, Polydore, I know not how to tell thee.
    Shame rises in my face, and interrupts
    The story of my tongue.

POLYDORE.   I grieve my friend
    Knows anything which he's ashamed to tell me;
    Or didst thou e'er conceal thy thoughts from Polydore? 345

CASTALIO.
    Oh, much too oft.
    But let me here conjure thee,
    By all the kind affection of a brother
    (For I am ashamed to call myself thy friend),
    Forgive me.   350

POLYDORE.
   Well, go on.
CASTALIO.
   Our destiny contrived
   To plague us both with one unhappy love.
   Thou, like a friend, a constant, generous friend,
   In its first pangs didst trust me with thy passion,   355
   Whilst I still smoothed my pain with smiles before thee,
   And made a contract I ne'er meant to keep.
POLYDORE.
   How!
CASTALIO.
   Still new ways I studied to abuse thee,
   And kept thee as a stranger to my passion—   360
   Till yesterday, I wedded with Monimia.
POLYDORE.
   Ah, Castalio! Was that well done?
CASTALIO.
   No, to conceal't from thee was much a fault.
POLYDORE.
   A fault! When thou hast heard
   The tale I'll tell, what wilt thou call it then?   365
CASTALIO.
   How my heart throbs!
POLYDORE.   First, for thy friendship, traitor,
   I cancel't thus— After this day, I'll ne'er
   Hold trust or converse with the false Castalio!
   This, witness Heav'n.
CASTALIO.   What will my fate do with me?
   I've lost all happiness, and know not why.   370
   What means this, brother?
POLYDORE.   Perjured, treacherous wretch,
   Farewell.
CASTALIO.   I'll be thy slave, and thou shalt use me
   Just as thou wilt— Do but forgive me.
POLYDORE.   Never!
CASTALIO.
   Oh, think a little what thy heart is doing;
   How, from our infancy, we hand in hand   375
   Have trod the path of life, in love together.

One bed has held us, and the same desires,
The same aversions, still employed our thoughts.
Whene'er had I a friend that was not Polydore's?
Or Polydore a foe, that was not mine?   380
Even in the womb we embraced; and wilt thou now,
For the first fault, abandon and forsake me?
Leave me amidst afflictions to myself?
Plunged in the gulf of grief, and none to help me?

POLYDORE.

Go to Monimia. In her arms thou'lt find   385
Repose. She has the art of healing sorrows—

CASTALIO.

What arts?

POLYDORE.   Blind wretch, thou husband! There's a question!

Go to her fulsome bed, and wallow there
Till some hot ruffian, full of lust and wine,
Come storm thee out, and show thee what's thy bargain—   390

CASTALIO.

Hold there, I charge thee—

POLYDORE.   Is she not a—

CASTALIO.   Whore?

POLYDORE.

Ay, whore— I think that word needs no explaining.

CASTALIO.

Alas! I can forgive ev'n this to thee;
But let me tell thee, Polydore, I'm grieved
To find thee guilty of such low revenge   395
To wrong that virtue which thou couldst not ruin.

POLYDORE.

It seems I lie then.

CASTALIO.   Should the bravest man
That e'er wore conquering sword, but dare to whisper
What thou proclaim'st, he were the worst of liars.
My friend may be mistaken.

---

397. *It seem I lie then*] The quarrel progresses in five stages of calculated insult to the lie direct, but the word *coward* precipitates the duel. Cf. Touchstone on the "seven degrees of the lie," *As You Like It,* V.iv.94 ff.

POLYDORE.   Damn the evasion!   400
   Thou mean'st the worst, and he's a base-born villain
   That said I lied.   [*Draws his sword.*]

CASTALIO.
   Do, draw thy sword, and thrust it through my heart!
   There's no joy in life, if thou art lost—
   A base-born villain—

POLYDORE.   Yes. Thou never camest   405
   From old Acasto's loins. The midwife put
   A cheat upon my mother, and instead
   Of a true brother, in the cradle by me
   Placed some coarse peasant's cub—and thou art he!

CASTALIO.
   Thou art my brother still.

POLYDORE.   Thou liest.

CASTALIO.   Nay then—   410
                                       He draws.
   Yet I am calm.

POLYDORE.   A coward's always so.

CASTALIO.
   Ah—ah— that stings home: coward!

POLYDORE.
   Ay, base-born coward—villain.

CASTALIO.
   This to thy heart then, though my mother bore thee.

They fight. Polydore *drops his sword, and runs on Castalio's.*

POLYDORE.
   Now my Castalio is again my friend!   415

CASTALIO.
   What have I done? My sword is in thy breast.

POLYDORE.
   So I would have it be, thou best of men,
   Thou kindest brother, and thou truest friend.

CASTALIO.
   Ye gods! We're taught that all your works are justice.
   Y'are painted merciful, and friends to innocence.   420
   If so, then why these plagues upon my head?

POLYDORE.
   Blame not the Heav'ns; here lies thy fate, Castalio.

Th'are not the gods, 'tis Polydore has wronged thee.
I've stained thy bed; thy spotless marriage joys
Have been polluted by thy brother's lust.   425

CASTALIO.
By thee—

POLYDORE.   By me, last night the horrid deed
Was done; when all things slept, but rage and incest.

CASTALIO.
Now, where's Monimia? Oh!

Enter Monimia.

MONIMIA.   I'm here! Who calls me?
Methought I heard a voice
Sweet as the shepherd's pipe upon the mountains,   430
When all his little flock's at feed before him.
But what means this? Here's blood—

CASTALIO.   Ay, brother's blood;
Art thou prepared for everlasting pains?

POLYDORE.
Oh, let me charge thee, by th'eternal justice,
Hurt not her tender life!

CASTALIO.   Not kill her? Rack me,   435
Ye powers above, with all your choicest torments,
Horror of mind and pains yet uninvented,
If I not practice cruelty upon her
And treat revenge some way yet never known.

MONIMIA.
That task myself have finished. I shall die   440
Before we part. I've drunk a healing draught
For all my cares, and never more shall wrong thee.

POLYDORE.
Oh, she's innocent.

CASTALIO.   Tell me that story,
And thou wilt make a wretch of me indeed.

POLYDORE.
Hadst thou, Castalio, used me like a friend,   445
This ne'er had happened; hadst thou let me know
Thy marriage, we had all now met in joy;
But ignorant of that,
Hearing th'appointment made, enraged to think

96

Thou hadst outdone me in successful love,   450
I in the dark went and supplied thy place;
Whilst all the night, midst our triumphant joys,
The trembling, tender, kind, deceived Monimia
Embraced, caressed, and called me her Castalio.

CASTALIO.

And all this is the work of my own fortune.   455
None but myself could e'er have been so cursed.
My fatal love, alas! has ruined thee,
Thou fairest, goodliest frame the gods e'er made,
Or ever human eyes and hearts adored.
I've murdered too my brother.   460
Why wouldst thou study ways to damn me further,
And force the sin of parricide upon me?

POLYDORE.

'Twas my own fault, and thou art innocent.
Forgive the barbarous trespass of my tongue;
'Twas a hard violence. I could have died   465
With love of thee, ev'n when I used thee worst;
Nay, at each word that my distraction uttered,
My heart recoiled, and 'twas half death to speak 'em.

MONIMIA.

Now, my Castalio, the most dear of men,
Wilt thou receive pollution to thy bosom,   470
And close the eyes of one that has betrayed thee?

CASTALIO.

Oh, I'm the unhappy wretch whose cursed fate
Has weighed thee down into destruction with him.
Why then thus kind to me?

MONIMIA.

When I'm laid low in the grave, and quite forgotten,   475
Mayst thou be happy in a fairer bride;
But none can ever love thee like Monimia.
When I am dead, as presently I shall be
(For the grim tyrant grasps my heart already),
Speak well of me, and if thou find ill tongues   480
Too busy with my fame, don't hear me wronged;
'Twill be a noble justice to the memory
Of a poor wretch, once honored with thy love.
How my head swims! 'Tis very dark: good night.   *Dies.*

CASTALIO.

    If I survive thee! What a thought was that!   485
    Thank Heav'n I go prepared against that curse.

Enter Chamont *disarmed, and seized by* Acasto, *and* Servants.

CHAMONT.

    Gape, Hell, and swallow me to quick damnation,
    If I forgive your house; if I not live
    An everlasting plague to thee, Acasto,
    And all thy race. Y'have o'erpowered me now;   490
    But hear me, Heav'n— Ah, here's the scene of death:
    My sister, Monimia! Breathless! Now,
    Ye powers above, if y'have justice, strike,
    Strike bolts through me, and though the cursed Castalio.

ACASTO.

    My Polydore.

POLYDORE.   Who calls?

ACASTO.   How cam'st thou wounded?   495

CASTALIO [*to* Chamont, *who goes to kneel by Monimia's body.*]

    Stand off, thou hot-brained, boistrous, noisy ruffian,
    And leave me to my sorrows.

CHAMONT.   By the love

    I bore her living, I will ne'er forsake,
    But here remain till my heart bursts with sobbing.

CASTALIO.

    Vanish, I charge thee, or—   *Draws a dagger.*

CHAMONT.   Thou canst not kill me;   500

    That would be kindness, and against thy nature.

ACASTO.

    What means Castalio? Sure thou wilt not pull
    More sorrows on thy aged father's head.
    Tell me, I beg you, tell me the sad cause
    Of all this ruin.

POLYDORE.   That must be my task;   505

    But 'tis too long for one in pains to tell.
    You'll in my closet find the story written
    Of all our woes. Castalio's innocent,
    And so's Monimia; only I'm to blame:
    Inquire no farther.

CASTALIO.   Thou, unkind Chamont,   510
    Unjustly hast pursued me with thy hate
    And sought the life of him that never wronged thee.
    Now, if thou wilt embrace a noble vengeance,
    Come join with me and curse.
CHAMONT.   What?
CASTALIO.   First thyself,
    As I do, and the hour that gave thee birth.   515
    Confusion and disorder seize the world,
    To spoil all trust and converse amongst men;
    'Twixt families engender endless feuds;
    In countries, needless fears; in cities, factions;
    In states, rebellion; and in churches, schism: 520
    Till form's dissolved, the chain of causes broken,
    And the Originals of Being lost.
ACASTO.
    Have patience.
CASTALIO.   Patience! Preach it to the winds,
    To roaring seas, or raging fires; the knaves
    That teach it laugh at ye, when ye believe 'em.   525
    Strip me of all the common needs of life,
    Scald me with leprosy, let friends forsake me,
    I'll bear it all; but cursed to the degree
    That I am now, 'tis this must give me patience:
    Thus (*stabs himself*) I find rest, and shall complain no
        more.   530
POLYDORE.
    Castalio! Oh!
CASTALIO.
    I come.
    Chamont, to thee my birthright I bequeath:
    Comfort my mourning father, heal his griefs—

        Acasto *faints into the arms of a servant.*

    For I perceive they fall with weight upon him.   535
    And for Monimia's sake, whom thou wilt find
    I never wronged, be kind to poor Serina.
    Now all I beg is—lay me in one grave,
    Thus, with my love. Farewell! I now am—nothing.

                      Dies.

CHAMONT.

    Take care of good Acasto, whilst I go   540
    To search the means by which the fates have plagued us.
      'Tis thus that Heaven its empire does maintain;
      It may afflict, but man must not complain.

                                         [*Exeunt omnes.*]

543. S.D. *Exeunt omnes*] *W1; om.*
Q1–4.

EPILOGUE

You've seen one orphan ruined here, and I
May be the next, if old Acasto die:
Should it prove so, I'd fain amongst you find
Who 'tis would to the fatherless be kind.
To whose protection might I safely go?   5
Is there amongst you no good nature? No.
What should I do? Should I the godly seek
And go a-conventicling twice a week?
Quit the lewd stage, and its profane pollution,
Affect each form and saintlike institution,   10
So draw the brethren all to contribution?
Or shall I (as I guess the poet may
Within these three days) fairly run away?
No; to some city lodgings I'll retire,
Seem very grave, and privacy desire,   15
Till I am thought some heiress rich in lands,
Fled to escape a cruel guardian's hands;
Which may produce a story worth the telling,
Of the next sparks that go a fortune-stealing.

1–2. *Orphan . . . I/May be the next*] The Epilogue is spoken by Serina (Mrs. Butler).

8. *conventicling*] accented on the third syllable; hence the innuendo and the pun. The report at the time was that the London apprentices were threatening "to pull down all the conventicle houses and bawdy houses in and about London," those in the suburbs of Moorfields and Whetstone Park being specified (*Calendar of State Papers, Domestic, 1679–1680*, p. 423).

13. *Within these three days*] before the third performance, the poet's day, in the event the play was damned.

19. *sparks . . . fortune-stealing*] Chamont inherits the whole of Acasto's estate, though he is hardly a "fortune-stealing spark" in the sense that Freeman, the ex-sailor, is. (Wycherley's *Plain Dealer* was first performed at Drury Lane in January, 1677.)

Appendix A

Racine, Otway, and Mrs. Barry

The Orphan has been called "the most Racinian of Otway's tragedies,"[1] and indeed, the "turns and counter-turns of emotion," the swift changes of mood, the elaborate interplay of sentiment and sensibility, and the comparative lack of physical action on stage, all suggest the influence of Racine, whose play *Bérénice* (1670) Otway had adapted in 1676 as *Titus and Berenice* (Dorset Garden, December). But if Otway treats of passions as overwhelming as those depicted by the great French dramatist, there is an essential difference. In reading *The Orphan*, one can only be oppressed by the sense of a very personal, a very subjective misery, an effect quite different from the sense of civilized "decorum" the French poet projects, along with an ethos which is more truly heroic.

Bonamy Dobrée speaks of *Venice Preserved* as being "continually marred by [Otway's] preoccupation with his personal troubles,"[2] but surely this is even more true of *The Orphan*. Indeed, the play lends some color of truth to the story of Otway's hopeless infatuation for the actress who created the part of Monimia, and to whom he allegedly wrote the despairing *Letters* first printed in 1697 with *The Familiar Letters of the Earl of Rochester*, the actress Elisabeth Barry.[3] If it is true that *The Orphan* had its inception before October 1678 and the outbreak of the Popish Plot,[4] then

---

1. Bonamy Dobrée, *Restoration Tragedy* (Oxford, 1929), p. 142.
2. Ibid., p. 144.
3. After Mrs. Barry's death in 1713, the printer Richard Wellington advertised a new edition of *The Familiar Letters*, identifying her as the recipient of the letters (R. G. Ham, *Otway and Lee* [New Haven, 1931], p. 83).
4. A. M. Taylor, "A Note on the Date of *The Orphan*," *Journal of English Literary History*, 12 (1945): 316–26. *The English Adventures*, the source of the play, was published in 1676.

the composition of the play coincides with this disastrous entanglement. By 1677 Mrs. Barry was already the mistress of the Earl of Rochester, the malicious and irresponsible patron to whom Otway in 1676 had dedicated *Titus and Berenice, with The Cheats of Scapin* (Term Catalogue, February), and whose lampoon of Otway, in *The Session of the Poets*, circulated anonymously in manuscript in October 1677. Mrs. Barry's daughter was born in December 1677,[5] and shortly thereafter Otway took a commission in the army and embarked for Flanders.[6] In April, just before his departure, his sardonic comedy, *Friendship in Fashion*, was produced at Dorset Garden, with Mrs. Barry in the role of Mrs. Goodvile.

It is possible to read too much into these circumstances, but it is impossible to escape the sense of Otway's too great personal involvement with the characters in *The Orphan*. If the contradictions now apparent in the play emerge from the web of Restoration "manners," perhaps the unresolved difficulties which critics have found in the plot derive in part also from the passionate bewilderment of the playwright *vis à vis* his own personal problems —unmitigated poverty, a noble and profligate patron who became his successful rival, and a hopeless infatuation for the actress who first established her fame in the part he created for her.

---

5. Henry Savile to the Earl of Rochester, 17 Dec. 1677 (*Hist. MSS Comm., The Marquis of Bath*, 2: 160).

6. Commission signed at Whitehall, 10 Feb. 1678 (Charles Dalton, *English Army Lists and Commission Registers, 1661–1714* [London, 1960], 1:208).

Appendix B

The Setting of *The Orphan*

Otway indicated no localized settings for *The Orphan*, and indeed there is no need for the changes of location, from "garden," to "saloon," and back again, which are given in the acting version published by John Bell in 1776, at a time when elaborate stage décor was coming into fashion. The action of the play can easily be envisioned as taking place in the courtyard, or on the terrace, of one of those Stately Houses of England which were built before the Civil Wars. Hatfield House, for instance, with its forecourt, flanked by wings, and its terrace overlooking a park at the rear, suggests a setting which the stage of the Dorset Garden playhouse could easily handle, with a minimum of "changeable scenery."

From a study of the various plays written for Dorset Garden, it appears that the stage of the playhouse was constructed so that two permanent proscenium doors opened onto the apron in front of the curtain, and that over each door was a permanent window. Hence, in Act III, the window of Monimia's apartment, and the entrance to it, offered no difficulty either to practice or to imagination. Behind each proscenium door, and the curtain, was a second permanent door, where the Page could eavesdrop (II.317), and through which Polydore could accidentally come upon Monimia and Castalio and overhear the appointment (III.286).[1]

According to Colley Cibber, actors preferred to speak their lines well out on the apron and close to the audience; hence the greater verisimilitude of the "asides," the greater believability of Chamont's failure to recognize Acasto at once in Act IV, and the

1. The arrangement of these doors at Drury Lane may be depicted in the frontispiece to *The Orphan*, printed for J. Darby, 1730.

necessity for the slow exits and entries as they are marked in the original text.

Given the permanent architectural features of the Dorset Garden playhouse, the production of *The Orphan* would require little or no "scenery." Any scenery that might be needed could be supplied economically by the "shutters" which were carried on the trolleys and the grooves that ran across the rear stage, parallel to the front curtain. These "shutters," or painted canvas flats, could slide back to "open" upon a small interior scene, or "close" upon it, so that the scenes were changed before the eyes of the audience, as Richard Southern has shown.[2] It is possible that these shutters were opened upon "Castalio lying on the ground" at the beginning of Act V. It is also possible that they obviated the apparently "false entry" for Monimia in Act IV, where Bell gives a direction for a change of scene to "a chamber," though it seems clear from the text that it is Monimia who returns to the place she left in order to find Castalio, and not Castalio who seeks out Monimia in her "chamber."

Since the curtain was raised at the beginning of the play, but presumably after the Prologue, and lowered only at the end, the Act divisions in performance were marked by the playwright's rhymed couplets, and more especially by the "Act Music," a long established convention.[3] The playwright had no need to mark the Act Music, since all the incidental music for plays was ordered either by the Prompter (in this case, John Downes), or by the Manager, who was Thomas Betterton, assisted by William Smith.

A quick curtain to bring an act to a close with a "tableau" was unknown to stage practice before the nineteenth century. In Otway's day, the Act Music covered the slow exits. The long speeches which bring the first four acts of *The Orphan* to a close may well have been spoken *through* "soft music," which continued while the actors walked off the stage, in full view of the audience. At the end of Act V, with three of the principals dead on the stage, and a fourth fainting in the arms of his attendants, it is not clear whether the stage direction "*Exeunt omnes*"[4] indicates that

---

2. *Changeable Scenery* (London, 1950), passim.

3. J. S. Manifold, *The Music in Drama, from Shakespeare to Purcell* (London, 1956), passim.

4. Given first in *The Collected Works*, 1712, and omitted in the first four quartos, where the word *Finis* at the end of the Epilogue seems to corroborate what Dryden says of the lowering of the curtain.

"the bearers" carried the corpses off stage before (or during) the speaking of the Epilogue, or that Serina spoke the Epilogue with the corpses in full view, as Dryden's Epilogue for *Tyrannic Love* suggests. From Dryden's Epilogue to *Sir Martin Mar-all*, it would appear that the curtain was lowered only after the Epilogue had been spoken.

Appendix C

Chronology

Approximate dates are indicated by *. Dates for plays are those on which they were first made public, either on stage or in print.

Political and Literary Events	Life and Works of Thomas Otway
1631 Death of Donne. John Dryden born.	
1633 Samuel Pepys born.	
1635 Sir George Etherege born.*	
1640 Aphra Behn born.*	
1641 William Wycherley born.*	
1642 First Civil War began (ended 1646). Theaters closed by Parliament. Thomas Shadwell born.*	
1648 Second Civil War. Nathaniel Lee born.*	
1649 Execution of Charles I.	
1650 Jeremy Collier born.	
1651. Hobbes' *Leviathan* published.	
1652 First Dutch War began (ended 1654).	March 3, Thomas Otway born; the son of Humphrey Otway, Rector of Woolbeding, Sussex.

1656
D'Avenant's *THE SIEGE OF RHODES* performed at Rutland House.

1657
John Dennis born.

1658
Death of Oliver Cromwell.
D'Avenant's *THE CRUELTY OF THE SPANIARDS IN PERU* performed at the Cockpit.

1660
Restoration of Charles II.
Theatrical patents granted to Thomas Killigrew and Sir William D'Avenant, authorizing them to form, respectively, the King's and the Duke of York's Companies.
Pepys began his diary.

1661
Cowley's *THE CUTTER OF COLEMAN STREET*.
D'Avenant's *THE SIEGE OF RHODES* (expanded to two parts).

1662
Charter granted to the Royal Society.

1663
Dryden's *THE WILD GALLANT*.
Tuke's *THE ADVENTURES OF FIVE HOURS*.

1664
Sir John Vanbrugh born.
Dryden's *THE RIVAL LADIES*.
Dryden and Howard's *THE INDIAN QUEEN*.
Etherege's *THE COMICAL REVENGE*.

1665
Second Dutch War began (ended 1667).
Great Plague.

Dryden's *THE INDIAN EM-
PEROR.*
Orrery's *MUSTAPHA.*

1666
Fire of London.
Death of James Shirley.

1667
Jonathan Swift born.
Milton's *Paradise Lost* published.
Sprat's *The History of the Royal
Society* published.
Dryden's *SECRET LOVE.*

1668
Death of D'Avenant.
Dryden made Poet Laureate.
Dryden's *An Essay of Dramatic
Poesy* published.
Shadwell's *THE SULLEN
LOVERS.*

Admitted as a Commoner of
Winchester College.

1669
Pepys terminated his diary.
Susannah Centlivre born.

Admitted as a Commoner of Christ
Church, Oxford (May).

1670
William Congreve born.
Dryden's *THE CONQUEST OF
GRANADA,* Part I.

1671
Dorset Garden Theatre (Duke's
Company) opened.
Colley Cibber born.
Milton's *Paradise Regained* and *Sam-
son Agonistes* published.
Dryden's *THE CONQUEST OF
GRANADA,* Part II.
THE REHEARSAL, by the Duke of
Buckingham and others.
Wycherley's *LOVE IN A WOOD.*

His father died (February).
Left Oxford without taking a degree
and sought a living in the London
theatrical world.

1672
Third Dutch War began (ended
1674).

Joseph Addison born.
Richard Steele born.
Dryden's *MARRIAGE A LA MODE.*

1674
New Drury Lane Theatre (King's Company) opened.
Death of Milton.
Nicholas Rowe born.
Thomas Rymer's *Reflections on Aristotle's Treatise of Poesy* (translation of Rapin) published.

1675
Dryden's *AURENG-ZEBE.*
Wycherley's *THE COUNTRY WIFE.**

ALCIBIADES produced by the Duke's Company at Dorset Garden in September.

1676
Etherege's *THE MAN OF MODE.*
Shadwell's *THE VIRTUOSO.*
Wycherley's *THE PLAIN DEALER.*

DON CARLOS produced at Dorset Garden in June, and *TITUS AND BERENICE* and *THE CHEATS OF SCAPIN* about December.

1677
Aphra Behn's *THE ROVER.*
Dryden's *ALL FOR LOVE.*
Lee's *THE RIVAL QUEENS.*
Rymer's *Tragedies of the Last Age Considered* published.

Attacked by Rochester in *A Session of the Poets.* (Otway believed Elkanah Settle to be the author.)

1678
Popish Plot.
George Farquhar born.
Bunyan's *Pilgrim's Progress* (Part I) published.

Military service in Flanders. Commissioned first as an ensign (February), then as a lieutenant (November).
FRIENDSHIP IN FASHION produced at Dorset Garden in April.

1679
Exclusion Bill introduced.
Death of Thomas Hobbes.
Death of Roger Boyle, Earl of Orrery.
Charles Johnson born.

Disbandment from the army (June).
THE HISTORY AND FALL OF CAIUS MARIUS produced at Dorset Garden in August or September.

111

1680

Death of Samuel Butler.
Death of John Wilmot, Earl of Rochester.
Dryden's *THE SPANISH FRIAR*.
Lee's *LUCIUS JUNIUS BRUTUS*.

THE ORPHAN (February or March) and *THE SOLDIER'S FORTUNE* (March) both produced at Dorset Garden.
The Poet's Complaint of his Muse published (February).
Awarded the degree of M.A. at Cambridge (September).

1681

Charles II dissolved Parliament at Oxford.
Dryden's *Absalom and Achitophel* published.
Tate's adaptation of *KING LEAR*.

1682

The King's and the Duke of York's Companies merged into the United Company.
Dryden's *The Medal, MacFlecknoe,* and *Religio Laici* published.

VENICE PRESERVED produced at Dorset Garden in February.

1683

Rye House Plot.
Death of Thomas Killigrew.
Crowne's *CITY POLITIQUES*.

THE ATHEIST produced at Dorset Garden (between June and November).

1685

Death of Charles II; accession of James II.
Revocation of the Edict of Nantes.
The Duke of Monmouth's Rebellion.
John Gay born.
Crowne's *SIR COURTLY NICE*.
Dryden's *ALBION AND ALBANIUS*.

Died April 14 in indigence on Tower Hill.

1687

Death of the Duke of Buckingham.
Dryden's *The Hind and the Panther* published.
Newton's *Principia* published.

1688

The Revolution.
Alexander Pope born.

Shadwell's *THE SQUIRE OF ALSATIA.*

1689

The War of the League of Augsburg began (ended 1697).

Toleration Act.

Death of Aphra Behn.

Shadwell made Poet Laureate.

Dryden's *DON SEBASTIAN.*

Shadwell's *BURY FAIR.*

1690

Battle of the Boyne.

Locke's *Two Treatises of Government* and *An Essay Concerning Human Understanding* published.

1691

Death of Etherege.*

Langbaine's *An Account of the English Dramatic Poets* published.

1692

Death of Lee.

Death of Shadwell.

Tate made Poet Laureate.

1693

George Lillo born.*

Rymer's *A Short View of Tragedy* published.

Congreve's *THE OLD BACHELOR.*

1694

Death of Queen Mary.

Southerne's *THE FATAL MARRIAGE.*

1695

Group of actors led by Thomas Betterton left Drury Lane and established a new company at Lincoln's Inn Fields.

Congreve's *LOVE FOR LOVE.*

Southerne's *OROONOKO.*

1696

Cibber's *LOVE'S LAST SHIFT.*

Vanbrugh's *THE RELAPSE.*

113

1697

Treaty of Ryswick ended the War of the League of Augsburg.

Charles Macklin born.

Congreve's *THE MOURNING BRIDE*.

Vanbrugh's *THE PROVOKED WIFE*.

His love letters to the actress Elizabeth Barry, Rochester's mistress, published in *Familiar Letters: Written by the . . . Earl of Rochester, and Several Other Persons of Honor and Quality*.

1698

Collier controversy started with the publication of *A Short View of the Immorality and Profaneness of the English Stage*.

1699

Farquhar's *THE CONSTANT COUPLE*.

1700

Death of Dryden.

Blackmore's *Satire against Wit* published.

Congreve's *THE WAY OF THE WORLD*.

1701

Act of Settlement.

War of the Spanish Succession began (ended 1713).

Death of James II.

Rowe's *TAMERLANE*.

Steele's *THE FUNERAL*.

1702

Death of William III; accession of Anne.

The Daily Courant began publication.

Cibber's *SHE WOULD AND SHE WOULD NOT*.

1703

Death of Samuel Pepys.

Rowe's *THE FAIR PENITENT*.

1704

Capture of Gibraltar; Battle of Blenheim.

Defoe's *The Review* began publication (1704–1713).

114

Swift's *A Tale of a Tub* and *The Battle of the Books* published.

Cibber's *THE CARELESS HUSBAND*.

1705

Haymarket Theatre opened.

Steele's *THE TENDER HUSBAND*.

1706

Battle of Ramillies.

Farquhar's *THE RECRUITING OFFICER*.

1707

Union of Scotland and England.

Death of Farquhar.

Henry Fielding born.

Farquhar's *THE BEAUX' STRATAGEM*.

1708

Downes' *Roscius Anglicanus* published.

1709

Samuel Johnson born.

Rowe's edition of Shakespeare published.

The Tatler began publication (1709–1711)

Centlivre's *THE BUSY BODY*.

1711

Shaftesbury's *Characteristics* published.

The Spectator began publication (1711–1712).

Pope's *An Essay on Criticism* published.

1713

Treaty of Utrecht ended the War of the Spanish Succession.

Addison's *CATO*.

1714

Death of Anne; accession of George I.

Steele became Governor of Drury Lane.
John Rich assumed management of Lincoln's Inn Fields.
Centlivre's *THE WONDER: A WOMAN KEEPS A SECRET.*
Rowe's *JANE SHORE.*

1715
Jacobite Rebellion.
Death of Tate.
Rowe made Poet Laureate.
Death of Wycherley.

1716
Addison's *THE DRUMMER.*

1717
David Garrick born.
Cibber's *THE NON-JUROR.*
Gay, Pope, and Arbuthnot's *THREE HOURS AFTER MARRIAGE.*

1718
Death of Rowe.
Centlivre's *A BOLD STROKE FOR A WIFE.*

1719
Death of Addison.
Defoe's *Robinson Crusoe* published.
Young's *BUSIRIS, KING OF EGYPT.*

1720
South Sea Bubble.
Samuel Foote born.
Steele suspended from the Governorship of Drury Lane (restored 1721).
Little Theatre in the Haymarket opened.
Steele's *The Theatre* (periodical) published.
Hughes' *THE SIEGE OF DAMASCUS.*

1721
Walpole became first Minister.

1722
Steele's *THE CONSCIOUS LOVERS*.

1723
Death of Susannah Centlivre.
Death of D'Urfey.

1725
Pope's edition of Shakespeare published.

1726
Death of Jeremy Collier.
Death of Vanbrugh.
Law's *Unlawfulness of Stage Entertainments* published.
Swift's *Gulliver's Travels* published.

1727
Death of George I; accession of George II.
Death of Sir Isaac Newton.
Arthur Murphy born.

1728
Pope's *The Dunciad* (first version) published.
Cibber's *THE PROVOKED HUSBAND* (expansion of Vanbrugh's fragment *A JOURNEY TO LONDON*).
Gay's *THE BEGGAR'S OPERA*.

1729
Goodman's Fields Theatre opened.
Death of Congreve.
Death of Steele.
Edmund Burke born.

1730
Cibber made Poet Laureate.
Oliver Goldsmith born.
Thomson's *The Seasons* published.
Fielding's *THE AUTHOR'S FARCE*.

117

Fielding's *TOM THUMB* (revised as *THE TRAGEDY OF TRAGEDIES*, 1731).

1731

Death of Defoe.

Fielding's *THE GRUB-STREET OPERA*.

Lillo's *THE LONDON MERCHANT*.

1732

Covent Garden Theatre opened.

Death of Gay.

George Colman the elder born.

Fielding's *THE COVENT GARDEN TRAGEDY*.

Fielding's *THE MODERN HUSBAND*.

Charles Johnson's *CAELIA*.

1733

Pope's *An Essay on Man* (Epistles I–III) published (Epistle IV, 1734).

1734

Death of Dennis.

The Prompter began publication (1734–1736).

Theobald's edition of Shakespeare published.

Fielding's *DON QUIXOTE IN ENGLAND*.

1736

Fielding led the "Great Mogul's Company of Comedians" at the Little Theatre in the Haymarket (1736–1737).

Fielding's *PASQUIN*.

Lillo's *FATAL CURIOSITY*.

1737

The Stage Licensing Act.

Dodsley's *THE KING AND THE MILLER OF MANSFIELD*.

Fielding's *THE HISTORICAL REGISTER FOR 1736*.